The House of Edelman

Aaron Edelman,
Watchmaker

Rose Edelman,
Saint

Herschel Edelman,
English & Dramatics Teacher,
called Morris Upside-Down
(Moishe Kapoyer)

having met in the Atlantic Ocean,
Rockaway, Long Island
and
married in the Bronx, New York

Ann Edelman,
Widow
of
Mr.
Everybody

David Edelman,
(deceased)
called Mr. Everybody
(famed T.V. Star),
also called Mamele
(Little Mother)—
for his dead grandmother—
in whose grave
he was born

The House of Mazeldich

Myron Mazeldich,
Rabbi

Deborah Mazeldich,
Saint

Netta Mazeldich,
called Pushky,
the Mah Jong Queen

Manny Mazeldich,
called Uncle Money,
the King of Junk

Moses Mazeldich,
called Stud Moses,
former Film-Star
and
United States
Vice-President

the *new* David Edelman,
also called Mamele
(Little Mother)—
born eight days ago in
his brother David's grave.

BRISBURIAL

a feast by

EDWARD POMERANTZ

MagiCircle PRESS

BRISBURIAL is published in limited edition only by
Magic Circle Press, 10 Hyde Ridge Road, Weston, CT 06883.

Library of Congress Catalog Card No.: 80-82714

ISBN 0-913660-13-2
ISBN 0-913660-14-0 pbk

For Eddie Geiges and Al Pomerantz
and for my friends and family

Throw away the lights, the definitions
And say of what you see in the dark

— Wallace Stevens

The Man With The Blue Guitar

The Helper

CHARACTERS

Herschel Edelman, called Moisḥe Kapoyer, Morris Upside-Down
Also: The Caterer
The Moyle

THE CHOSEN FAMILY

nmanuel (Manny) Mazeldich, called Uncle Money, the King of Junk

Netta Edelman, called Pushky the Mah Jong Queen

loses Mazeldich, called Stud Moses, rmer movie-star, Senator, ıd United States Vice-President

David Edelman, called Mamele, an infant, eight days old

he Widow

he Commentator

he Soldier, attendant to Stud Moses

r. Doover, attendant to Uncle Money

da Grosbart, Pushky's lady-in-waiting

Mourners/Feasters

A Television Crew

The Students of Henry Ford Junior High

The Henry Ford Trio

A Chicken

SETTING

A small wooded cemetery on a hill. Up center — an enormous gravestone marked EDELMAN — surrounded by smaller graves and scattered trees. At the entrance to the cemetery — a large marquee reading: TODAY — AT THIS CEMETERY — THE BRISBURIAL OF MAMELE EDELMAN. Dwarfing the cemetery — three monster billboards with mammoth blow-ups of the personalities they advertise: Up center — to the right of the gravestone: MR. EVERYBODY IS ANYBODY YOU WANT HIM TO BE. EVERY NIGHT AT 8. CHANNEL 12 Down left: HAVE *YOU* GONE DOWN FOR GOD YET? GO ALL THE WAY — WITH STUD MOSES. Down right: WHY BE A HUMPTY DUMPTY? LET UNCLE MONEY PUT YOU BACK TOGETHER AGAIN — UNCLE MONEY'S USED PARTS — STRAIGHT AHEAD. (UNCLE MONEY's smiling face — smoking a cigar — is superimposed onto HUMPTY's). Between the billboards and surrounding the cemetery from the highway on all sides are lesser signs reading DAIRY KING: TRY MY FROZEN STICK. IT WILL MELT IN YOUR MOUTH; MOTEL DREAMLAND, DEER CROSSING; ASK FOR MAGIC FINGERS AT YOUR NEXT STOP; YIELD; PAY TOLL 1,000 FEET; SQUEEZE RIGHT; SOFT SHOULDERS; ONE WAY; VACANCY; NO VACANCY; HEATED POOL; AIR-CONDITIONED; STATE POLICE; SAUNA; ACCIDENT AHEAD; DETOUR; CONSTRUCTION; DIM LIGHTS; TURN OFF RADIO; SCENIC ROUTE, etc. All the signs are going in different directions. Between and above them are mountains of junk and dead cars — through which we can barely see sky.

TIME

The near future.

(No curtain. Thrust stage. Twilight. Sound of cars on highways from all directions. As the audience seats itself, a MAN *runs on; early 50's, ravaged and wild-eyed, seized with panic, his hands and overcoat stained with blood. He stops, seeing us, then comes forward.)*

MAN

Where is it? Where did I leave it? What did I do with it? Where did I put it?

(Searching through pockets, pulling things out)

Lists... Keys... It never ends... First the generator... now the switch... Brisburial for the good of the country... Mamele Edelman born in the grave... Gotta stop... Keep it running... Breath-death. Then only click. Click-click. Then only the clock. Ticking... ticking... Still ticking... Gotta stop... Keep it running...

(A PROFESSIONAL MOURNER *comes on dressed in a ratty suit and takes a seat on a down left gravestone.*

MAN

Rushing to MOURNER:)

Where is it? It wouldn't start... I held it in my hand... Cut up like a chicken...

MAN (cont'd)

(The MOURNER *looks at him, pulls his arm away, takes out a prayer-shawl and skull-cap and puts them on)*

Ice-cold. The blood still warm. Always late. Shitting in a fox-hole...

(The MOURNER *takes out a hard-boiled egg and cracks it against the tombstone)*

The more you schtup, the more it eats...

(The MOURNER *starts to rock back and forth in silent prayer, peeling and eating the egg.*

The MAN *goes down to members of the audience as they take their seats)*

Never enough... Never satisfied... Over and over... Around in circles...

(A YOUNG MAN *runs on, around 19, lean and watchful.* HE *stops, finding the* MAN*)*

Gotta stop. Keep it running. Stop, you die. Dead, you're free.

(The YOUNG MAN *comes up slowly, carefully behind him)*

Gotta schtup. Find a space. Where is it? What did I do with it?

(Searching through pockets)

Lists. Keys. I want what's coming. I want what's mine.

(A knife falls out. HE *stops, terrified, looks out at audience)*

Go away... Go back to the beginning. The scene of the crime. What crime? Clean as a knife. To stop the schtupping... Break the circle... Gotta stop. Ticking... Ticking...

MAN (cont'd)

(To the YOUNG MAN:)

Where is it? Where did I leave it? What did I do with it? Where did I put it?

(Going off)

Lists. . . Keys. . . One missing. . .

(HE *exits.)*

The YOUNG MAN *looks after him, then turns to the audience and smiles. With his eyes still on us,* HE *picks up the knife.*

Offstage, sounds of PEOPLE *arriving: cars, equipment, voices, footsteps. The* YOUNG MAN *snaps the knife shut. A final smile, then* HE *goes off after the* MAN.

Slowly, gradually, the stage begins to fill. First, a camera dollies in. Then The COMMENTATOR *comes on, testing his microphone, adjusting his makeup. Then the* MOURNERS *start to arrive — down the aisle and from over the hill — each one eventually stopping at the center gravestone to place a rock upon it, then take his place in the circle around it)*

OLD MAN IN WHEEL CHAIR

(Wheeled on by his SON; *loudly)*

What time does the assassination go on, George?

GEORGE

There is no assassination today, Dad. We're at the cemetery.

OLD MAN

What the hell are they having an assassination at a cemetery for?

GEORGE

They're not. It's your cousin Mamele's brisburial.

OLD MAN

Bris what?

GEORGE

Burial.

OLD MAN

If they're burying him, what the hell are they giving him a bris for?

GEORGE

They're not. They're circumcising his brother.

OLD MAN

His mother! What the hell are they circumcising **her** for?

GEORGE

Not his mother. His brother.

OLD MAN

Whose brother?

GEORGE

Mamele Edelman's. Mr. Everybody.

OLD MAN

Mr. Who?

GEORGE

Everybody.

OLD MAN

I thought everybody was dead.

GEORGE

He **is** dead. His brother Mamele was just born.

OLD MAN

When?

GEORGE

Last week. Right here.

(Indicating grave)

In the grave. Where the first Mamele was being buried.

(The OLD MAN *looks at his* SON *suspiciously. The* SON *covers his* FATHER *with a blanket. The* FATHER *slaps his hand)*

ROSE

(Coming on with her thirteen-year old son, RONALD)

You know something, Ronald? My whole family is here.

SIMON

(Coming down the aisle, talking to ANOTHER MAN)

All of a sudden I'm yelling at the maid because she's putting my pillow on the wrong side off the bed...

ROSE

(Continued, to RONALD)

I feel more at home here than I do at home.

*(*SHE *reaches into pocket-book, gives the* PROFESSIONAL MOURNER *some change and goes to greet* GEORGE *and the* OLD MAN.

The PROFESSIONAL MOURNER *begins to wail, rocking back and forth.* RONALD *takes out a yo-yo and starts to swing it)*

SIMON

Yesterday my kid sits in my chair at the dinner-table. I almost murdered him. . .

(A YOUNG MAN *with a beard and hand-held movie-camera comes on accompanied by his Vogue* GIRLFRIEND, *who carries his light meter)*

YOUNG MOVIE-MAKER

(Running over to PROFESSIONAL MOURNER)

Don't move. . . Just be natural. . .

SIMON

I don't even remember choosing that seat, that side of the bed. . .

SOPHIE

(Coming on with her twelve-year old DAUGHTER, *who carries a life-size doll the exact replica of herself)*

Kim, wait. . .

SIMON

It just happened. . .

SOPHIE

(Stopping at gravestone, to KIM)

I have to tell you something. . .

SIMON

Like getting married...

SOPHIE

In the beginning, I loved your father very much...

SIMON

Going into the dress business.

(HE *stops at gravestone, places rock upon it, takes his place in the circle)*

SOPHIE

In the end, he loved me long after I had stopped.

GEORGE

(Standing at MR. EVERYBODY's *grave, addressing it)*

Poor son-of-a-bitch.

SOPHIE

(Continuing, to KIM)

Never, not once, did we ever love each other equally or at the same time...

(SHE *weeps softly, goes to gravestone)*

GEORGE

(Continued, addressing grave)

That's a hundred grand a week laying in there.

ROSE

(Addressing gravestone)

Mr. Everybody...

(Suddenly lights start to flash and the camera zooms in)

SOPHIE

Oh my God. We're going to be on television.

(SHE *starts to put on make-up and primp her* DAUGHTER.

The YOUNG MOVIE-MAKER *runs over to film her. She poses with one arm around the gravestone)*

ROSE

Every night he was anybody you wanted him to be... Your mother... your father... your boss... your boyfriend...

GEORGE

You have any idea what he was worth an hour?

ROSE

There wasn't anything you couldn't say to him...

GEORGE

Twenty grand a day.

ROSE

The way he looked at you...

GEORGE

Just laying there...

ROSE

Saying the same things over and over...

GEORGE

You have any idea what he was worth a minute?

(THE COMMENTATOR *turns on a switch connected to the gravestone.* MR. EVERYBODY's *voice speaks to us)*

MR. EVERYBODY'S VOICE

I'm sorry... Forgive me... Why didn't you tell me?

(ROSE *looks up as if the* VOICE *has come from heaven. As* MR. EVERYBODY continues his litany, she repeats everything he says, while TELEVISION *cameras and* MOVIE-MAKER *go in and out amongst the* CROWD. *A* WOMAN *comes on and looks around furtively, then takes out some pills and swallows them down. Her* HUSBAND *comes on and looks at her, disgustedly, reaches out his hand. She gives them to him, and he spills them on the ground. All during the litany, there is a steady stream of* MOURNERS, PEOPLE TAKING PICTURES *of* PEOPLE TAKING PICTURES, MOURNERS *and* FEASTERS *greeting, consoling, snubbing each other)*

MR. EVERYBODY (and **ROSE**)

(Continued, without stopping, no emotion)

If I had only known... it isn't all my fault... it isn't all your fault... we're only human... cry, if you want to... get it off your chest... there's nothing to be ashamed of... everything'll be all right. Say anything you want... Curse, if you want to... This is between you and me... nobody can hear you... Who's judging?... Who am *I* to judge?... There are things beyond us... things we can't control... Try to see it from my point of view... You're absolutely right... I was absolutely wrong... Why didn't you say so?... This never would have happened.... I'm sorry... Forgive me... I forgive you...

(By now, the stage is full and the CREW *is ready. The lights dim and the* COMMENTATOR *is given his cue)*

COMMENTATOR

(Low-key, dignified, in the midst of the action)

Good evening...

ROSE

It isn't all your fault... it isn't all my fault...

OLD MAN

What time does the assassination go on, George?

COMMENTATOR

You are about to participate in the first live satellite coverage of the first brisburial known to man...

GEORGE

Sixty-five cents a second. Can you beat that?

COMMENTATOR

The brisburial of Mamele Edelman...

(Suddenly the CATERER *runs on, thick mustache and bushy eyebrows, wearing a uniform and cap, and winding a pocket-watch)*

CATERER

(Out of breath, looking around, interrupting COMMENTATOR, *as if he isn't there)*

What time is it? Am I late?... You'll never believe what happened to me. ...

CATERER (cont'd)

(HE *runs off again, revealing the back of his uniform which reads:* FANTASY CATERERS)

COMMENTATOR

(Going on, bewildered)

The joining together of two of the world's most ancient and sacred rites... Circumcision and Burial...

(The CATERER *runs on again, pulling an overloaded U-haul-it wagon, over the top of which we can see ladders, an enormous many-tiered cake, punch bowl, candelabras; on top of it all, the* CATERER'S HELPER, *in identical uniform, sitting on a throne, wearing Harpo wig and exaggerated nose)*

THE CATERER

(To audience, into camera)

My car wouldn't start... Forty dollars on a new generator. It wasn't the generator at all. It was the starter-switch. For $1.50... Did you ever hear such a thing?

(HE *runs back to wagon and snaps his fingers.*

The HELPER *jumps off and they begin to unload)*

SOPHIE

Who's that?

SIMON

Sssh. The caterers.

COMMENTATOR

(Going on, flustered)

For the benefit of those members of our live and satellite audience who are not Jewish...

OLD MAN

(Belligerently)

What did he say? What did he say about the Jews?

CATERER

(Coming down, to audience, going on with story)

No sooner did I fix the switch, my windshield wiper went.

(HE *returns to the wagon)*

COMMENTATOR

Bris is the ritual act of circumcision...

(HELPER *pulls out huge axe and begins to sharpen it)*

CATERER

The whole way I had to keep rubbing, blowing...

COMMENTATOR

Practiced by the Jewish people. . .

OLD MAN

What did he say? What did he say about the Jews?

COMMENTATOR

Eight days after the birth of the male child...

CATERER

(Spreading tablecloth over center gravestone, then placing candelabras at each end)

CATERER (cont'd)
All of a sudden coming toward me...

COMMENTATOR
To commemorate his covenant with Abraham...

CATERER
A station wagon on top of a Volkswagen. . .

COMMENTATOR
The first Hebrew...

OLD MAN
What did he say? What did he say about the Hebrews?

COMMENTATOR
. . . whose son Isaac was the first to be circumcised. . .

(The HELPER *begins to sharpen very close to* COMMENTATOR)

CATERER
Before I realized they were on a delivery truck I was already over the divider skidding through a Howard Johnson's into a Kentucky Fried Chicken...

(The HELPER *tests his axe by snipping off the* COMMENTATOR's *tie. The* CROWD *gasps)*

COMMENTATOR
(Finishing his sentence)
... on the eighth day...

OLD MAN
Anti-Semite...

CATERER

(To COMMENTATOR)

You never saw such a mess...

(HE *and* HELPER *return to wagon.*

During the following interchange, the CATERER *fills a small salt-shaker with an enormous bag of salt, eventually burying it, while the* HELPER *fills an enormous pepper-grinder, one pepper-corn at a time)*

COMMENTATOR

(Trying to restore order, pretending everything is fine)

What more fitting way to complete the burial of Mamele Edelman...

CATERER

I'd've been here sooner but they wouldn't let me on the turnpike again without a car...

COMMENTATOR

... known to the world and worshipped by millions as Mr. Everybody...

CATERER

I had to wait for a trailer to come by...

COMMENTATOR

... than to perform and celebrate this ancient rite right here...

CATERER

So I could run alongside it with nobody seeing me...

COMMENTATOR

. . . with the bris of his infant brother . . .

CATERER

At least I didn't have to look for a parking space . . .

COMMENTATOR

The *new* Mamele . . .

CATERER

Every night the same cycle . . .

COMMENTATOR

. . . born here eight days ago . . .

CATERER

Mondayswednesdaysfridays . . . tuesdaysthursdayssaturdays . . .

COMMENTATOR

. . . as a symbol of man's eternal powers of renewal and regeneration . . .

CATERER

8 to 11 . . . 11 to 2 . . .

(CATERER *and* HELPER *go to wagon, start to set up elaborate punch-bowl with a naked boy Bacchus statue standing over it)*

COMMENTATOR

Especially today . . .

CATERER

Every pump — your heart beats like a dog . . .

COMMENTATOR

. . . at this grave hour . . .

CATERER

68,000 miles and where have I been?

COMMENTATOR

. . . of national despair. . .

CATERER

Around the block. . .

COMMENTATOR

. . . and trembling world leadership. . .

CATERER

(Plugging in punch bowl)

At least a dog gets relief. . .

(The naked Bacchus starts to pee punch into the bowl. CATERER *and* HELPER *go to wagon, take out ladders, and begin to string up a banner from tree to tree)*

COMMENTATOR

Already demoralized by another presidential scandal and the resumption of fighting in Southeast Asia. . .

CATERER

The other day my friend Myron says to me confidential nobody should hear: Tell the truth. You happy?

COMMENTATOR

. . . as well as the mysterious explosion of another shipment of nerve gas 200 miles from Denver. . .

CATERER

Sure I said: What's happy?. . . A little money. . . Good health. . . all the appliances. . .

COMMENTATOR

All it took was the mysterious death of one of its most beloved television stars...

CATERER

Just last week... they all broke...

(The banner goes up now: FANTASY CATERERS... LET US CATER YOUR NEXT AFFAIR... EAT YOURSELF SICK... THAT'S WHAT YOU'RE HERE FOR... WHAT'S MONEY... DON'T THINK ABOUT IT. JUST EAT... WAKES... WEDDINGS... BAR MITZVAHS OUR SPECIALTY!!!)

COMMENTATOR

(Going on)

... his mutilated body discovered by his father at this very spot...

CATERER

The dish-washer... the dryer... the can-opener... the pencil-sharpener...

COMMENTATOR

... to catapult an entire nation into its worst Depression since the 1930's...

OLD MAN

Watch. Some poor yid'll get blamed for it...

CATERER

I called my electric man...

COMMENTATOR

Even *with* the government's assurance that the war's outcome is definitely inevitable and that the nerve gas, although lethal, has no side-effects...

CATERER

His machine was out of order.

*(*CATERER *and* HELPER *go to wagon, unload three thrones, and place them around center grave)*

COMMENTATOR

Unlike its economic predecessor, however, *this* Depression is largely psychological...

CATERER

The other night I woke up in a sweat... where's my laundry ticket?

COMMENTATOR

... one might even say, spiritual...

CATERER

Two o'clock in the morning and I'm turning over drawers...

COMMENTATOR

In many ways, the country has never been so well off...

CATERER

Who had a ticket?

(CATERER *and* HELPER *go to wagon, set up plank, roll down an enormous many-tiered cake to corner of stage)*

COMMENTATOR

Higher wages... higher profits...

CATERER

Just today... blood all over the sidewalk...

COMMENTATOR

Increased government spending... increased consumption...

CATERER

A young boy, afraid his father, a gonsa furrier, would find out he was flunking, ran into the bank, grabbed the guard's gun, and shot himself in the mouth...

COMMENTATOR

Yet somehow... somewhere...

CATERER

Some people have all the luck...

COMMENTATOR

Something seems to have gone wrong...

CATERER

The bullet went through *him* and killed the window-cleaner outside...

(HELPER *nudges him.*

To audience)

Don't think about it. Just eat.

(HE *and* HELPER *remove top half of cake. Out pops a teen-age* NEGRO GIRL *carrying a platter of chopped liver, followed by a procession of other* NEGRO *and* PUERTO RICAN TEENAGERS, *each holding a tray of*

CATERER (cont'd)

food: hors d'oeuvres consisting of chopped liver, gefuilte fish, knishes, and fruit salad. Behind them: a TEEN-AGE TRIO, *also* NEGRO *and* PUERTO RICAN, *made up of trumpet, bongos, and bass.*

To crowd, audience)

You like chopped liver? Gefuilte fish?

(The BOYS *and* GIRLS *go amongst the crowd and into the audience serving the food)*

COMMENTATOR

(Quickly, in a daze now, trying to retain his sanity, reading the cue-cards)

Whether it's the increase in crime and random violence here at home...

CATERER

Here. Have a knish.

COMMENTATOR

... or the wars of liberation spreading and erupting everywhere...

CATERER

My mother's recipe...

COMMENTATOR

Every other second...

CATERER

Not this canned stuff you get in a jar...

COMMENTATOR

No one can put his finger on it . . .

(HELPER *stuffs food into* COMMENTATOR's *mouth)*

CATERER

Good? Delicious? . . . You haven't tasted anything yet . . .

COMMENTATOR

(With a mouthful)

All the people know is that their bellies are full and so are their pockets . . .

CATERER

(Holding up tray)

My fantasy of fresh fruit . . .

COMMENTATOR

But *where,* they're asking . . .

CATERER

Mamele Balls!

COMMENTATOR

Are our leaders?

CATERER

Cut from canteloupe in season.

COMMENTATOR

What kind of future are we creating for our children?

(The stage and audience are suddenly flooded with the glare of oncoming headlights)

CROWD

Here they come... Pushky... The baby... Money... Stud.

OLD MAN

What time does the assassination go on, George?

CATERER

(To audience)

Eat. Eat. That's what you're here for.

*(*HE *signals to* HELPER *and* THEY *disappear into audience)*

COMMENTATOR

(Recovering)

Mamele Edelman's family, ladies and gentlemen... Mr. Everybody's remarkable mother, Mrs. Netta Edelman, who only lask week — throwing herself into the grave of her dead son in an effort to follow him, brought on the delivery of her *second* son, thus becoming the only woman in history to give birth in the grave, not once, but twice...

CROWD

She's getting out... She has the baby...

COMMENTATOR

Never before has history so dramatically or bizarrely repeated itself. As you all know, Mr. Everybody was born in the grave himself twenty-eight years ago — when his mother, pregnant and beside herself with grief, jumped into the grave of her dead mother — in an effort to follow *her*.

CROWD

There's Money... There's Stud...

COMMENTATOR

For over a week now, the FBI has been investigating the mystery of Mr. Everybody's death, the discovery of his muti-

COMMENTATOR (cont'd)

lated body in the very grave in which he was born... while an anxious nation has waited by its television sets — to find out if Mrs. Edelman — known to her friends as Pushky, the Mah Jong Queen — and her *new* son Mamele — born prematurely by two months — would live...

CROWD

Make room... Stand aside...

(Suddenly a screen is lowered, blocking our view of the FAMILY's *entrance)*

COMMENTATOR

Before we meet this extraordinary woman and her Chosen Family, here are the first live on-the-scene-satellite shots of that incredible birth...

(Movie begins: Same scene as on the stage. Cameras, MOURNERS, FAMILY *around grave. Only this time, a coffin is being lowered into the grave as a* RABBI *stands over it saying a prayer. Suddenly, a* WOMAN *rushes forward, hysterical, screaming, struggles against the efforts of her family to hold her back, breaks through, and jumps into the grave.*

While this portion of the film is being shown, the CATERER *and* HELPER *re-appear and feed the audience)*

CATERER

What are you worried about?... You'll diet tomorrow... Don't think about it... Just eat... Did you see this?

(Takes out clipping)

CATERER (cont'd)

The front page of the New York Times... Pope absolves Jews of role in crucifixion... Down at the bottom: Kosher tuna poisons Irish family in Queens... Can you win? You're just like I am... I eat and eat... I can still go a little something... Don't think about it... Just eat...

(Suddenly the film goes berserk. Everyone running backwards and forwards at an accelerated pace — DOCTORS, *stretchers,* MOTHER *and* CHILD *being raised from grave, people fainting, general pandemonium)*

COMMENTATOR

We seem to be experiencing some technical difficulty, if you'll just...

CROWD

Pushky... Pushky darling!!

(All at once, the TRIO *begins to play* The Hatikvah *— the Jewish National Anthem — and the screen is raised to reveal* MRS. NETTA EDELMAN, PUSHKY *the Mah Jong Queen, behind it. A small, buxom woman in her late 40s, she sits in a wheelchair, flanked on one side by her brother* STUD MOSES, *a "larger-than-life" movie star in his early fifties; on the other by her brother,* UNCLE MONEY, *also exaggerated, either very skinny or very fat, around 55. Behind her, a* WOMAN *of her own age, a sister mah-jong player, veiled in black, attending her.* STUD *and* MONEY

have their attendants, too: the SOLDIER, *accompanying* STUD; DR. DOOVER — *a small Chinese in a doctor's white jacket, accompanying* MONEY.

In PUSHKY's *arms, her blanketed infant.*

As soon as SHE *appears, the* CATERER *and* HELPER *disappear.*

During the following song, PUSHKY *is wheeled downstage center, as* MEMBERS OF THE CROWD make way for her, burst into tears, kneel at her feet, try to touch her, the baby, MONEY *and* STUD)

ONE OF THE NEGRO TEEN-AGE GIRLS

(Singing to the melody of The Hatikvah)

When I was single I had nothing to do
I sat by my window lacing up my shoe
Then I got married I had so much to do
I had so many children I didn't know what to do.
One cried mama, put me into bed.
The other cried papa, gimme a piece of bread.
Mama... Papa... All day long they cry to you...
Now they are gone...
I don't know what to do.

COMMENTATOR

(Off to the side)

Mrs. Edelman has just arrived...

WOMAN IN CROWD

(Arthritic, trembling, rushing forward,

WOMAN IN CROWD (cont'd)

clutching and kissing both PUSHKY *and the baby)*

Pushky... Pushky sweetheart... let me touch you... God love you...

COMMENTATOR

Accompanied by her two brothers...

OLD MAN

Where's the father?

SOPHIE

(Rushing forward, pulling DAUGHTER *and doll)*

Stud... Stud, it's me... Your cousin Sophie...

COMMENTATOR

Mamele's godfathers, Stud Moses...

ROSE

Manny, it's me... your cousin Rose...

COMMENTATOR

and Uncle Money... two of the nation's most unique and influential figures...

SOPHIE

(To STUD)

Remember? Playing Doctor behind my father's candy store...

ROSE

(To MONEY)

Remember? The one who used to save you everything?

COMMENTATOR

Reunited for the first time in years by this tragic and joyous event.

SOPHIE

I always knew you'd go places.

ROSE

String... rubber-bands... burned-out bulbs... the foil from chewing-gum...

COMMENTATOR

Stud Moses Mazeldich...

SOPHIE

(Pushing DAUGHTER *and doll in front of* STUD)

My daughter...

ROSE

(Pushing RONALD *in front of* MONEY)

My son...

COMMENTATOR

Ten years ago, just another Hollywood has-been...

SOPHIE

(Displaying daughter)

The youngest Miss Subways ever...

ROSE

(Displaying son)

The head of Student Government...

COMMENTATOR

Then overnight — the popular idol of a whole new generation of Late Show watchers — going on to even greater glory as United States Senator — and our first Jewish Vice-President...

SOPHIE

(Pushing daughter forward)

Eleven and a half...

ROSE

(Pushing son forward)

Just bar-mitzvahed...

(SOPHIE *takes out poster from handbag and unravels it: A large picture of her* DAUGHTER; *underneath:* MISS SUBWAYS. KIM ROSENBAUM. EAGER, SENSITIVE, AND BLONDE, KIM STILL WAITS FOR HER MISSING-IN-ACTION FATHER TO RETURN FROM KOREA. OTHER INTERESTS: DATING, PLAYING WITH DOLLS, SERIOUS MODELING.

ROSE *takes out Bar-Mitzvah picture of her* SON, *blown-up, dressed in tallis and skull-cap.*

As they display the pictures, the COMMENTATOR *goes on)*

COMMENTATOR

(Going to MONEY)

Manny Mazeldich, ladies and gentlemen... former peddler and used-parts dealer... known the world over — as Uncle Money, the King of Junk...

SOPHIE

Go, darling, go. Show Uncle Stud how you make a living...

(SHE pushes DAUGHTER *forward with doll)*

ROSE

(Pushing RONALD *forward)*
Tell Uncle Money all about Queer's Day. . .

(SOPHIE *pulls the string of her* DAUGHTER's *doll — or her* DAUGHTER, *we're not sure which)*

DOLL-CHILD

Hello. . . I'm your bad little girl.

RONALD

I got this idea. Friday's Queer's Day.

DOLL-CHILD

Don't yell at your own little girl. Yell at *me!*

RONALD

Anybody who isn't wearing purple that day is an automatic queer.

DOLL-CHILD

Don't punish her. Punish *me!*

RONALD

I figure purple's a good color. Nobody wears it much.

DOLL-CHILD

Don't hit her. Hit *me!*

RONALD

The whole night I was up dying. . .

DOLL-CHILD

Go ahead. I can take it.

RONALD
Purple socks, ties, and handkerchiefs.

DOLL-CHILD
I'm made of steel.

RONALD
Then I sold them.

DOLL-CHILD
I know you don't love me... that there are times you wish you never had me...

RONALD
in the second-floor boy's room...

DOLL-CHILD
Enjoy your guilt!

RONALD
... for a quarter a piece.

DOLL-CHILD
Hit *me*... Punish *me*... Yell at *me*...

RONALD
You'd be surprised how many kids don't want to be queer...

DOLL-CHILD
(Broken, repeating itself)
See if *I* care... See if *I* care... See if *I* care...

RONALD
A lot of teachers, too...

(SOPHIE *tries to fix the* DOLL-CHILD, *hitting it in frustration)*

(ROSE *pats her* SON *proudly.)*

COMMENTATOR

(Trying to recoup, make order again)

Mrs. Edelman... Uncle Money... Stud... If I may... Seldom does an entire country have the opportunity to meet such an extraordinary, indeed, such a Chosen Family... Uncle Money... Is it true you're completely recovered now?

MONEY

Completely... Absolutely... Completely...

COMMENTATOR

(To audience)

As you all know, this is Uncle Money's first public appearance since his incredible operation...

SIMON

(Running to MONEY *from* CROWD)

Manny... It's *me*... Simon...

COMMENTATOR

Two years ago, the victim of a head-on collision in Rio de Janeiro...

SIMON

I hear you know the President...

COMMENTATOR

where he had gone in the face of a revolution to protect his enormous holdings in diamonds and pears...

SIMON

Tell him... Tell him we're not all intellectuals...

COMMENTATOR

he so seriously suffered damage to all his major limbs and

COMMENTATOR (cont'd)

organs it was doubtful anyone could save him...

SIMON

(Taking out and unwrapping something)

Show him this...

COMMENTATOR

(Crossing to DR. DOOVER)

However, thanks to the painstaking dedication of Dr. Toshira Doover...

SIMON

A new organization...

COMMENTATOR

Uncle Money has made one of the most miraculous recoveries in medical history...

SIMON

(Displaying skull-cap)

The Red, White and Blue Yarmelkes...

COMMENTATOR

becoming the first completely transplanted man to ever survive...

SIMON

(Giving MONEY *a yarmelke)*

Tell him the next war he can count on us... I'm the leader...

MONEY

(To CROWD, *displaying his hands, his body)*

Completely... Absolutely... Completely...

(DR. DOOVER *gives* MONEY *a shot.*

SIMON *gives out yarmelkes to the* CROWD)

COMMENTATOR

(Going to STUD)

And *you,* Stud... How are *you* feeling?

STUD

Never better.

COMMENTATOR

Amazing. . .

(To audience)

Just last November... defeated in his campaign for the Presidency and stricken with terminal cancer of the groin, Stud Moses made one of the most fantastic comebacks in Show Business history...

STUD

Nothing fantastic about it... When you've got God for a doctor...

COMMENTATOR

(To audience)

Convinced that he was miraculously cured and that his healed penis is the direct connection between God and a poor suffering humanity, he abandoned his political career to devote himself exclusively to healing and saving the world. . .

(To STUD*)*

Tell us, Stud... Having just come back from a triumphant tour of the war, how did you find the boys' morale over there?

STUD

Here's one of the boys right here. Why don't you ask him?

COMMENTATOR

Hi, soldier. Welcome home...

SOLDIER

It's good to be here.

COMMENTATOR

I'll bet it is. Especially today at Mamele Edelman's brisburial.

SOLDIER

(Testifying)

Stud Moses is doing a wonderful job. Not only for his own. But for the entire world.

COMMENTATOR

Really...

SOLDIER

You believe it! Up until Stud Moses showed up, we were nothing but a bunch of limp peckers.

COMMENTATOR

Wonderful... wonderful...

SOLDIER

(Going on, undaunted, into cameras, almost in a trance)

Then outa nowhere... just like it used to be in one of his movies... there he was... just standing there autographing helmets... the shit flying all around him... bombs, bullets, mines... blowing up everywhere... frying some of us like chickens... and *him,* not even flinching... just standing there autographing... saying... You too can live forever... Just sign up and go down for God...

COMMENTATOR

That's very interesting.

SOLDIER

You believe it... At first, some of us were skeptical just like

SOLDIER (cont'd)

you are... But then Ollie Robbins, he went first... Then all of us... Till each one comes running out of that tent like there was no tomorrow... yelling: Let me at em... Let me at em... Jumping over mines like they was vegetable patches... shooting up whole villages... women... kids...

COMMENTATOR

Thank you very much...

SOLDIER

I tasted Glory, understand? With my own eyes, I saw it rise and rise again to fill our guts with God... No shame, either. Just natural... like each of us was virgin and this was sacred duty...

COMMENTATOR

(Breaking away)

Mrs. Edelman... Pushky... Would *you* mind answering a few questions?

IDA (PUSHKY's *lady-in-waiting)*

(Protecting PUSHKY)

You want to know something, talk to *me*. I'll tell you anything you want to know.

COMMENTATOR

Who are you?

IDA

Ida Grosbart. 4731 Pelham Parkway. Apartment 7K... Ever since he was this high I knew him.

COMMENTATOR

Who?

IDA

The first Mamele. Mamele Edelman. Mr. Everybody. Who else?

COMMENTATOR

According to the records, his name was David.

IDA

For Deborah. His grandmother's name.

PUSHKY

(Suddenly crying out)

Mama... I'm sorry... Take me with you...

IDA

(Consoling her)

It's all right, darling... It's only the television...

(To COMMENTATOR)

What else do you want to know?

COMMENTATOR

If his name was David, why did they call him Mamele?

IDA

That was his name. Mamele... Little Mother!!!

PUSHKY

(Again, at the sound of her mother's name)

I'm sorry. What did I do wrong?

IDA

(Patting PUSHKY, *to* COMMENTATOR)

What else should they call him?

COMMENTATOR

I see. And the name Pushky...

IDA

You ever play Mah Jong? Poker? Canasta?

(COMMENTATOR *keeps shaking his head no)*

Pushky's the pot... the winnings... what the game is all about.

COMMENTATOR

Do you mean to say Mrs. Edelman has never lost?

IDA

Sure she's lost. But never... never... in all the years I'm playing... and I'm playing a lot of years now... did she ever lose a pot without winning back double...

PUSHKY

(Crying out, holding out infant)

I'll make it up to you... I promise...

IDA

It's all right, darling. . . Sha. . .

(Removing mah jong tiles from her bag)

Two bam... three crack...

(PUSHKY *fingers the tiles, smiles, relaxes, rubs and slides them together over the baby's head...)*

COMMENTATOR

(To audience)

The brisburial of Mamele Edelman, ladies and gentlemen... For those of you who are tuning in late... the burial of the *first* Mamele — Mr. Everybody... joined together with the

COMMENTATOR (cont'd)

circumcision of his brother — the *new* Mamele — born eight days ago — to celebrate man's eternal powers of renewal and regeneration...

(To the FAMILY)

Stud... Money... Wouldn't you say it's unusual to celebrate a bris at a cemetery?

MONEY

Nothing unusual about it.

STUD

The first feasts and festivals were all held in cemeteries.

MONEY

Whenever people got together to honor their dead.

STUD

Besides, who's usual?

(A YOUNG WOMAN *in her middle-to-late twenties appears, very pregnant, and walks through the* CROWD *to the gravestone where she takes out a banana and starts peeling it)*

CROWD

The wife... The widow... Pushky's daughter-in-law... The wife... the widow... Pushky's daughter-in-law...

COMMENTATOR

Mr. Everybody's widow, ladies and gentlemen...

OLD MAN

Where's the father?

COMMENTATOR

Since the death of her husband, withdrawn and mute, refusing to speak to anyone, even members of her husband's family...

(The WIDOW *drops the banana peel in the grave and walks past* PUSHKY, *the baby, and the* BROTHERS *to the downstage corner, eating the banana. The* CROWD *gasps, looks away in shame)*

Tell us, Stud, ... Money... Rumors have been circulating that you both plan to make a dramatic announcement today. Will this have any bearing on the solution of your nephew's murder?

STUD

Who said it was murder?

COMMENTATOR

According to the police, the nature of the mutilation was such that it seems unlikely anyone could have done such horrible violation to himself.

MONEY

What do the police know?

STUD

Why would anybody want to murder him?

MONEY

Why would he want to kill himself?

COMMENTATOR

Well, if he did kill himself, how would you explain the absence of a weapon, in this case, an axe or very sharp knife.

STUD

Perhaps he buried it.

MONEY

Maybe it was stolen.

COMMENTATOR

But the first person to discover his body was his father.

OLD MAN

Where *is* his father?

STUD

Before that.

COMMENTATOR

You mean somebody who came upon his body and took it?

MONEY

Exactly.

COMMENTATOR

But why?

STUD

To protect the real murderer.

MONEY

Create confusion.

STUD

Perhaps a scavenger.

MONEY

A bum. Finding something to hock.

COMMENTATOR

But then how do you explain the disappearance of his childhood diary? His tape-recorder? Both missing from his home.

STUD

Coincidence.

MONEY

Conspiracy.

STUD

Any number of possibilities.

COMMENTATOR

But the phone call to his father that night: Meet me at the cemetery... the scene of the crime...

MONEY

Ask his father...

STUD

If you can find him.

PUSHKY

(Crying out)

Moishe Kapoyer...

IDA

Is he *ever* here?

(Suddenly commotion from the aisles: The MOYLE *running through the audience, dressed in long black robes with long beard and sideburns, thick foggy glasses, his head and shoulders covered with prayer-shawls. Behind him, his* ASSISTANT, *dressed in iden-*

tical clothes and beard, carrying a satchel)

MOYLE

(Squinting, out of breath, winding his watch)

What time is it? Am I late? You'll never believe what happened to me...

IDA

(Finishing sentence)

Always with the head somewhere else...

OLD MAN

Is that him?

GEORGE

Who?

OLD MAN

The father?

IDA

(Going on)

Never where it belongs... Upside-down.

GEORGE

No. The moyle.

OLD MAN

What the hell is *he* doing here?

MOYLE

(On stage now, squinting, searching)

Where's the mother? Where's the boy?

COMMENTATOR

The moyle, ladies and gentlemen... The professional circumciser here to perform the new Mamele's bris.

MOYLE

(Stops, to audience)

My whole car sank. Plop. Right in the middle of the highway.

(During the following story, the MOYLE *and his* ASSISTANT *prepare for the ritual. The* ASSISTANT *unpacks his satchel and throws the* MOYLE *everything he removes, including a book entitled:* CIRCUMCISION: INSTRUCTIONS FOR BEGINNERS; *a pair of garden shears, barber scissors, butcher's cleaver, tweezer, vize, a plane, a ratchet, an electric drill, a saw, a needle and thread, thimble, sewing machine, magnifying glass, skewers, etc., all of which the* MOYLE *spreads on the gravestone)*

MOYLE

Fortunately, on the other side... Ajax Repairs... My luck, Ajax wasn't in... His mechanic was. If you ask me, they all come from the same greasy womb... A helpless moyle on his way to a bris plop in the middle of a highway and he wants *I* should bring the car to *him*... Did you ever hear such a thing?... If I could bring the car to him what would I need to bring the car to him for? ... I called the AAA. Would they come?

(Reaches into pockets, pulls out clippings, letters, chalk, rubber-bands, finally reading, squinting:)

MOYLE (cont'd)

Dear Sir... Due to your excessive use of the club's emergency road service facilities we have no alternative but to cancel your membership...

(Crumples letter)

Every afternoon the drop-outs take the air out of my tires... I sit there like a schmuck waiting for the Automobile Association of America to come and fill me up... If it isn't drop-outs, it's junkies ripping out your battery cable or the cold freezing up your testicles into figs every morning, they expect an old Chevy to go off like a rocket...

(Looking around, squinting)

Where's the father? Where's the grandparents?

(Spotting COMMENTATOR)

You...

(Pulls out pen and certificate)

Be a witness...

(He gives the COMMENTATOR *the pen; it leaks.*

The COMMENTATOR *gives it to* MONEY *who gives it to* STUD. *They keep passing it back and forth trying to get rid of it as the* MOYLE *returns to gravestone where his* ASSISTANT *helps him into surgical gown and gloves.*

Being dressed:)

My wife the pony-player. Every night she wraps her killing in the tin foil... the baggies... Then she locks it in the freezer — between the lamb chops, the Birds Eye... Lately, after supper, she likes a visit in the south...

(Shrugs)

At least I get to think a little, even pray... Who has time anymore?

(Uncorks wine and pours it)

MOYLE (cont'd)

Kaiser the kosher butcher... Every morning like clockwork — out of the shop and into the manicurist...

(Takes a swig, rolls it around in his mouth, spits it out)

Then over to the chiropractor to get his stomach muscles relaxed. . .

(Pours another)

I said to him: Kaiser, your son-in-law is stealing from the till... Who cares, he says to me... As long as I have clean nails every morning... and a long shit!

(Holds up glass, begins to doven)

MONEY

Who is this man?

STUD

I thought you hired him...

MOYLE

The congregation will please lower their heads and repeat after me... Hear O Israel the Lord our God the Lord is One. . .

(EVERYONE *looks at each other in confusion, then obeys)*

CONGREGATION

Hear O Israel the Lord our God the Lord is One. . .

MOYLE

Praise be the Lord to whom all praise is due forever and ever...

CONGREGATION

Praise be the Lord to whom all praise is due forever and ever...

MOYLE

Bend down on one knee and rise up...

OLD MAN

What did he say?

MOYLE

Bend down on one knee and rise up... Bend down... Rise up... Bend down... Rise up...

(A FEW *of the* MOURNERS *try to obey; find themselves doing calisthenics)*

MONEY

What's going on around here?

MOYLE

Praised be the Lord for giving us occasion to praise him. Praised be the Lord for giving us occasion to mourn. Praised be the Lord for giving us occasion to mourn without which we would have no occasion to congregate... Eat and drink... Drink and eat...

(The HELPERS *fill the cups and glasses of the* CROWD, SOME *of whom drink.* OTHERS *pass out food,* SOME *eat)*

Praised be the Lord for giving us our daily death. Praised be the Lord for giving us our daily death without which there would be no void... Praised be the Lord for giving us this void without which we would have no appetite... Praised be the Lord for giving us this appetite without which we would have no children... Praised be the Lord for giving us our children without whom we could not answer death...

(To HELPERS *and* CONGREGATION)

MOYLE (cont'd)

Empty. Fill up. . . Empty. . . Fill up. . .

(HELPERS *pour wine again and serve food)*

We will now honor those members of the family and congregation who in the past year have answered death for the last time:

(Here begins a list of names that should last as long [if not longer] as anyone can take. While he is reciting them, the CONGREGATION *mutters and prays for their dead.*

Reciting)

Mildred Kirsch, Shelley Zimmerman, Marty Schwartz, Rebecca Baumgarten, Ziggie Adler, Joseph Berman, Roger Gans, Moe Guss, Fanny Dryer, Arthur Ginsberg, Anna Friedman, Bessie Rae, Dr. Harold Frankenberger, Bertha Fine, Robert Goodman, Danny Diamond, Sonia Loeb, Harry Leff, William Straus, Emil Israel, Sara Siegel, Marilyn Rosenbaum, Harry Buxbaum, Louis Shemitz, Rose Stutsky, Rochelle Greene, Julie Hamerman, Abraham Kramer, Minna Kleinberg, George Tucker, Seymour Karp, Leon Resnick, Paul Chernoff, Freda Perlman, Natalie Ostrow, Hilda Jacobson, Belle Rosen, Edward Resnikoff, Jack Aptheker, Herbert Horowitz, Kate Yudkin, Nathan Martinson, Bella Martinson, Barney Martinson, Barry Martinson, Gert Hochman, Hennie Slepowitz, Albert Shapiro, Leonard Gershon, Pinky Herman, Adelaide Selinkoff, Alexander Davidson, Bobby Owens, Eugene Schisgal, Ida Levine, Rhoda Markowitz, Amy Resnick, Elaine Levy, Louis Lovell, Minna Meyer, Rosalind Greenflower, Jacob Rusky, Jacob Rothenberg, Tillie Fiedler, Edwin Starkist, Ben Straub, Rita Mishkin, Doris Katz, Dr. Saul Jacoby, Rabbi Sam Grossinger, Blanche Silverman, Debbie Krassner, Izzie Zepp. . .

MOYLE (cont'd)

(HE *drinks. Then to* HELPERS *and* MOURNERS*)*

Empty... Fill up... Empty... Fill up...

(Wine is poured again. Also food)

We will now cut our garments and cover ourselves with ashes to symbolize our grief and guilt.

(The HELPERS *give out scissors and urns. The* CONGREGATION *looks perplexed. The* HELPER *shows them what to do by ripping the clothes of some of the* MOURNERS *and throwing ashes in their faces)*

O living fountain... source of all healing... all life... we thank Thee for creating the fruit of the vine. Blessed art Thou O Lord our God King of the universe for creating the fruit of the vine and for cutting it down...

(To HELPER)

Cut from the blood-stained tree under which the first son was mutilated a branch and place it upon the altar to signify the completion of burial...

(HELPER *cuts down overhead branch with leaves on it)*

Blessed art Thou O Lord our God King of the Universe for cutting down this branch from our vine and giving us another in its place... Blessed art Thou O Lord our God King of the universe for giving us this new branch whose flesh we cut to satisfy Thy hunger. Blessed art Thou O Lord our God King of the Universe for giving us this new branch whose blood we flow to quench Thy thirst...

(To CONGREGATION*)*

Drink up and bring forth the second son...

(MONEY *and* STUD *go to take child from* PUSHKY)

MOYLE (cont'd)

O Lord O holiest of hosts we thank Thee for this great feast... O Lord O Shepherd we thank Thee for making of this grave a great stomach which receiveth and which yieldeth back. . .

(MONEY *and* STUD *tug at child.* PUSHKY *clutches at it, not letting it go.* IDA *helps to release it.* MONEY *and* STUD *tug at it themselves, then with dignity, carry it together back to* MOYLE)

Sing praises unto the grave for it hath done marvelous things...

PUSHKY

(Bewildered, her arms empty)

Where are you going, mama?... Why are you leaving me?

MOYLE

Shout unto the grave Thy praises and embrace it with open arms...

PUSHKY

I'm sorry, Mama. . . Whatever I did, I'm sorry. . .

MOYLE

Sing for joy unto the grave with offerings and the sound of trumpet...

(Trumpet begins)

PUSHKY

(Shouting)

I won, Mama. . . Every time the pushky is full, I win!

MOYLE

Yes, with offerings and the voice of drums...

(Wild primitive Jewish jazz begins. As MOSES *and* MONEY *hold the infant before the dovening* MOYLE, *the* TRIO *leads a dance around the grave, circling each* MOURNER *until he makes an offering. At first,* THEY *are scared and hesitant, then they begin to contribute with fever and contagion.* ONE *throws in a shoe,* ANOTHER *a ring. Then: loose change, dollar bills, wallets, contact lenses, chewing gum, anklet bracelets, a mink coat, cigars, pills, keys, etc. During the offerings, the following things may be heard.*

"The ring is from me, darling, Aunt Marilyn..." "If you see my father, tell him to go to hell..." "That's from me buddy. Don't say I never gave you anything..." "We miss you on television, dear..." "What time does the assassination go on, George?"... "Here... [throwing in a cigar] ... Take two. One for you ... One for God..." "If this doesn't keep you warm, nothing will..." "You should live and be well..." "We're proud of you, kid..." "As long as you have your health..." "Where's the father? ..."

As each offering is completed, EACH MOURNER *goes back to his place in the circle and claps and stamps his feet to the music. The* MUSICIANS *now circle around* PUSHKY)

CROWD

Come on, Pushky... Show 'em how...

(Slowly, with dignity, PUSHKY *rises, despite* IDA's *efforts to hold her back. Then suddenly* SHE *bursts into dance as the* CROWD *cheers and eggs her on)*

That's showing 'em... I knew she could do it... Give 'em one for us, darling... *That's* our Pushky... They don't make 'em like that anymore...

(The WIDOW *stands in front of* PUSHKY. *They confront each other.*

MUSIC *suddenly stops)*

MOYLE

Present the child for circumcision.

(MONEY *and* STUD *hesitate; the* HELPER *takes the child from their arms)*

O Lord our God God of our fathers Abraham Isaac and Jacob bless this child who was conceived as an answer to death...

(HELPERS *start to put gown on* MONEY *and* STUD, *tying them from behind)*

He who is conceived as an answer to death is holy. He who is conceived as an answer to death is holy and must be fed...

(HELPERS *bring platters of chopped liver, gefuilte fish and knishes to* MOYLE's *side)*

Before we feed this holy child — the honored mother and blessed godfathers will please step forth and partake of the food to insure its worthiness of the child's palate.

(PUSHKY, STUD, *and* MONEY *step forward. The* HELPER *gives the* MOYLE *the special platter)*

O Lord, O God — may this honored mother and these blessed godfathers...

OLD MAN

Where's the father?

(The MOYLE *stops, gives the* OLD MAN *a dirty look, goes on)*

MOYLE

May they never know from hunger.

(Feeding PUSHKY)

Open... Close...

(Feeding and choking STUD)

You should live and be well.

(Feeding and choking MONEY)

As long as you have your health...

(The MOYLE *goes to the child)*

O Lord, Oh God, He who is conceived as an answer to death is the source of all nourishment...

(Stuffs child with chopped liver.

MONEY *and* STUD *attempt to stop him, realize they are restricted by the ties of the gown)*

MOYLE (cont'd)

He who feeds this child who is an answer to death feeds God.

(Stuffs child with knish)

He who feeds this child who is an answer to death feeds himself...

(Stuffs him with fish)

He who feeds this child who is an answer to death feeds death...

(Stuffs again)

He who is conceived as an answer to death must be fed until God and Death are satisfied...

(Stuffs again)

God is never satisfied...

(Stuffs again)

Neither is Death...

(Stuffs again)

He who does not recognize death as the source of all nourishment does not recognize God...

(Stuffs again)

Without Death, there is no Fear... Without Fear, there is no God...

(Stuffs again)

Death is the Father of God...

(Baby is taken by HELPERS)

Sing praises unto Death as ye would to God for they are one and the same thing...

(HELPER *hands* MOYLE *knife.* STUD *and* MONEY *try to do something; the* HELPERS *hold them back.*

MOYLE

(Head bowed, the knife high)

O Lord, O Death, hear our sins before we make this child clean for Thee... He who repents now will be cleansed and born again...

(*The* CROWD *looks at each other, confused and scared. The* MOYLE waits. They begin to murmur confessions: "Sorry, God... I just can't help myself, God... Forgive me, God... I don't believe in you, God... God help me, God... I don't know what comes over me, God... I love him, God... He disgusts me, God... Get me out of this, God... I hate myself, God!!! ")

MOYLE

O Lord, O Death... if ever Thou were to give me guidance, bless me now in the guidance of this hand...

(HELPERS *open the infant's blanket and stand in front of it, giving the appearance that they are holding the baby down. The* MOYLE *squints and aims, then he slowly brings the knife down, his hand trembling. Just as he reaches the baby, he snaps his fingers and one of the* HELPERS *hands him a clamp. With a sudden abrupt movement, he clamps the child's penis as though he were catching a fish. Then he starts to apply the knife and suddenly stops, snapping his finger again. The* HELPER *flashes a light on the baby, the* MOYLE *squints. The* OTHER HELPERS *gather around to have a quick look and consultation. The* MOYLE *snaps his fingers for the manual, the* HELPER *gives it to him, he looks something up, throws the manual away. Through all this, the* CROWD *is murmuring: What's the matter?... What's happening?... What's he doing?... Who* is *he?... What's wrong?... I can't look... Tell me when it's over... Call a doctor... Call the police..." The* MOYLE *snaps his fingers, the* HELPER *gives him a magnifying glass, the* MOYLE *squints, looks through it, buries his head in the blanket so that we can only see his hands snapping his fingers for more instruments, larger and larger magnifying glasses, which he keeps flinging away. Finally, popping up:)*

MOYLE

Incredible!

(Ducks down again)

PUSHKY

The baby... Something's wrong with the baby!

MOYLE

(Popping up again)

Where's the father?

PUSHKY

Oh my god...

CROWD

What's wrong? What does he want the father for?

MOYLE

I demand to see the father!

PUSHKY

(Swaying)

Mamele... Mamele...

CROWD

Where is he? . . . Where's Morris?

MOYLE

(To STUD)

You. . . Are you the father or aren't you?

(To MONEY)

You. . . Who are you?

PUSHKY

I'm sorry, Mama. . . I'm sorry. . . Whatever I did, I'm sorry. . .

MOYLE

I never heard of such a thing. Is there a father or isn't there?

STUD & MONEY

What's wrong? What do you need the father for?

(DR. DOOVER *and* SOLDIER *start for baby; they're stopped by* HELPERS)

CROWD

Some father. . . Is he *ever* here?. . . Was he *ever* there?. . . Moishe Kapoyer. . . Morris Upside-Down. . .

MOYLE

What's wrong?

*(*HE *holds up baby)*

You call this a joke? What's the meaning of this?. . . This is no little boy. . . It's a little girl. . .

*(*HE *squeezes it)*

It *feels* like a little girl. . .

(Squints)

It *looks* like a chicken!

(Reaching into blanket, HE *pulls out a dead, blood-dripping chicken with the*

MOYLE (cont'd)

doll-head of an infant on it. As the CROWD *gasps and* PUSHKY *screams:)*

It *is* a chicken!

(The doll-head falls off. PUSHKY *collapses. The* MOYLE *flings the chicken away)*

What's going on here? Don't tell me... I wouldn't stay to listen.

Starts off, pulling off shawls)

MONEY

Stop him. . .

STUD

Where's he going?

MONEY

Don't let him get away.

(HELPERS *stop the* CROWD, *standing in front of them, forming a barricade. The* MOYLE *stops center, removing his skull-cap)*

MOYLE

Circumcising chickens. . .

*(*HE *spits)*

You should be ashamed of yourselves...

(Taking off robes, revealing caterer's uniform underneath)

If *I* was the father, I wouldn't be here either. . .

(Pulls off long beard, revealing caterer's bush moustache)

Some people have all the luck...

MOYLE (cont'd)

(Pulling off mustache, revealing his true face, that of the man who opened the play)

Mondayswednesdaysfridays...

CROWD

It's him... The father... Moishe Kapoyer!

MOYLE

(Stepping out of his uniform)

tuesdays...thursdays...saturdays...

PUSHKY

(Quietly, intensely)

The baby...

MOYLE

(Naked now, except for boxer shorts — with banner hanging down the front marked DADDY*)*

At least a dog gets relief...

PUSHKY

(Screaming)

What have you done with the baby?

(HELPERS *restrain her, force* STUD *and* MONEY *into thrones)*

MOYLE/CATERER/MORRIS

(Standing there, being helped into overlong, many-pocketed, blood-stained overcoat he wore at beginning)

What time is it? Am I late? You'll never believe what happened to me...

MONEY

Okay, brother-in-law...

STUD

Start explaining...

MORRIS

(Explaining, incoherently, as if it makes perfect sense)

My car wouldn't start... Forty dollars on a new generator ... It wasn't the generator at all... It was the starter-switch. For $1.50...

PUSHKY

He's crazy... He's gone out of his mind...

MORRIS

Did you ever hear such a thing? ... A whole son. Cut up like a chicken...

PUSHKY

The police... Call the police...

(PEOPLE IN THE CROWD *start to run for it, the* HELPERS *stop them)*

MORRIS

Calls me in the middle of the night: Hello, pa. I'm pregnant... My own son. Knocked up. Wants *me* to be the father...

PUSHKY

(To STUD *and* MONEY*)*

Do something!

MORRIS

Me. His own father.

MORRIS (cont'd)

(Going to PEOPLE *in crowd, explaining)*

Meet me at the cemetery, he says. . . The scene of the crime. . . What crime? The crime of my birth. . .

PUSHKY

(Rocking back and forth, weeping)

Mamele. . . Mamele. . . What has he done to you?

MORRIS

I'm coming, I told him. Soon as I get the car started. . . Every morning — ten minutes. . . In the cold — a half-hour. . .

PUSHKY

His car. . . His car. . . Always his car. . .

MORRIS

By the time I got there. . . you never saw such a mess. . *Pieces* everywhere. . . A nose. . . His cock. . .

(PUSHKY *puts her hands to her ears and shakes her head violently)*

MONEY

That's enough, Goddamnit.

STUD

Where's the kid?

(MORRIS *looks at them, then down at his hands. A moment, then he lets out a cry and covers his eyes.* PUSHKY *signals* STUD *and* MONEY. STUD *signals the* SOLDIER — *who makes a run for it)*

HELPER

(Stopping SOLDIER *with knife)*

I wouldn't do that...

(The SOLDIER *goes back to place)*

PUSHKY

(Quietly, to MORRIS)

Moish, please... Give me the baby.

MORRIS

(Looking up, bewildered, quietly)

What baby?

PUSHKY

(Quietly)

Our son David.

MORRIS

Whose son? *Which* son?

PUSHKY

The *new* Mamele.

MORRIS

(Agitated again, going around in circles)

Old Mameles... New Mameles... Around in circles...

(Stopping)

What did I do with it? Where did I put it?

(To HELPER)

I can't remember. I can't keep track...

HELPER

(Quickly)

Here. Chew this.

(Taking out a piece of thread)

HELPER (cont'd)
It'll help you remember...

CROWD & PUSHKY
Who's that? Who's he?

MORRIS
Who are you?

HELPER
One of your students.

MORRIS
What students?

HELPER
Henry Ford Junior High. The school where you teach.

MORRIS
Teach what?

HELPER
English and Dramatics... You asked for my help to finish what you started.

MORRIS
Started what?...

(HE walks away, agitated)

I have no starter-switch.

HELPER
(To CROWD)

He's forgotten who he is...

(To PUSHKY)

If you want your baby, we have to help him remember... Step by step... Just like a baby...

HELPER (cont'd)

(HELPER *goes to* PUSHKY *and pulls a thread off her dress.*

PUSHKY *looks at* HELPER, *bewildered. The* HELPER *goes to corner, puts a shawl around himself and starts rocking back and forth — making believe he's threading a needle*

Singing quietly to himself)

When I was single, I had nothing to do. . . I say by my window lacing up my shoe. . .

(MORRIS *looks up)*

MORRIS

Mama!

HELPER

(Smiling gently at MORRIS)

Herschel, darling, come here. I want to sew your button.

(HE *resumes humming,* MORRIS *goes to him)*

Here. . .

(HE *gives* MORRIS *thread)*

Chew this. . .

(MORRIS *looks at thread, bewildered)*

MORRIS

(To HELPER)

You're not my mother. . .

HELPER

I'm trying to help you remember. . . when you were a little boy

HELPER (cont'd)

and she sewed a button on you, she always gave you a piece of thread to chew on so you wouldn't lose your memory.

MORRIS

How do *you* know that?

HELPER

You told me all about it. It's a Jewish superstition.

MORRIS

What do *you* know from Jewish?

HELPER

I know what you told me.

MORRIS

Goy. Filthy genital. My mother was a saint.

HELPER

I know. You told me.

MORRIS

How dare you put her in your mouth? How dare you live while my chicken lies cut?

HELPER

(Correcting him)

Lays.

MORRIS

Who's the teacher here? You or me?

HELPER

(Correcting him)

I.

MORRIS

Raise your hand if you've got something to say.

(The HELPER *raises his hand, holding the thread)*

Goddamn smartasses. They think they know everything.

*(*HE *grabs the thread and starts chewing)*

My mother was a saint... My father shit all over her...

PUSHKY

It's working... He's remembering...

MORRIS

Seven kids he gave her. Did she even know I was alive? ... Hello, ma. Hersch. Wait. I'll see if he's home... Fat prick. When did he have time? Always in his watches in the back of the store. Did he ever look up? Say a kind word? A bum in the street. All he wanted was a nickel. Get the hell out of here. Go to work like *I* did... Work. Work. That's all she saw from him. Down on her knees... never a penny... Strangers off boats he'd feed like armies. *Us,* he'd starve... Did she ever speak up? Take my part? ... Father Time, they used to call him... Squinting in his beard, his watches... Ticking... ticking... What was inside? The way God thinks? 108 fever it took to kill him. I'm melting, he cried. At last, some words. What did he leave us? Cough drops. Tweezers. It served her right. She got what she deserved. Women are for laying, cooking, suffering... They don't want to work, kick 'em in the ass...

(To HELPER)

What's in this stuff?

HELPER

Your whole life.

MORRIS

(Spitting thread out)

Forget it.

*(*HE *walks away, sits.* MONEY *and* STUD *urge* PUSHKY *to approach him, quietly.* SHE *goes to him.)*

PUSHKY

Moish, darling. Be reasonable.

MORRIS

To HELPER)

Who's the hen?

HELPER

Your wife Pushky.

MORRIS

She's got big tits.

STUD

I'm warning you, brother-in-law...

MORRIS

(To HELPER, *indicating* STUD *and* MONEY*)*

The cock. And bull?

HELPER

Her two brothers.

MORRIS

They look sick. Put some fat on them.

(HELPERS *go to* STUD *and MONEY and stuff their mouths with food.)*

PUSHKY

(Desperately)

Where is he?

MORRIS

(Looking around, then back to PUSHKY)

Who?

PUSHKY

The chicken.

MORRIS

(Rising, indignant)

Are you accusing me of stealing your chicken, madam?

(Aside, to audience, like Groucho)

I've robbed a few cradles in my lifetime, but *this* is insane.

*(*HE *Grouchos away)*

PUSHKY

Maniac! Give me my baby!

MORRIS

(Spinning around, himself again)

What baby? What's the rush?

(To audience)

The minute we're married, she wants a baby. Her mother — dying . . . She can't wait . . .

PUSHKY

The *first* Mamele. . . He's beginning to remember. . .

STUD

(To HELPER)

Thread.

MONEY

More thread.

(The HELPER *gives* MORRIS *more thread)*

PUSHKY

Keep remembering.

MORRIS

(Chewing)

They take me in the Army, she's still not pregnant... In the Pacific — a letter: You're gonna be a father... How? When? Was I ever there? ...Seven months later — a son. A Mamele! I'm shitting in a foxhole... He's born in a grave!

(HELPER *snaps his fingers and the* HELPERS *bring down a high-chair. The* HELPER *gets into it, playing the first Mamele)*

HELPER

(Dressed like Mamele, holding a candle)

Hot? Candle? Candle hot?

PUSHKY

What is he doing? What's going on here?

MORRIS

I come home from the war, he's still in the high-chair. Four years old. One Candle.

(To PUSHKY*)*

Four years old? Going on two?

(PUSHKY *looks at him, distracted, then at the* HELPER, *then back to MORRIS.*

A moment then:)

PUSHKY

(Playing along, acting out the past)

You couldn't make it for his first birthday, so I postponed it a little. Is that a crime? Four years, the war took out. They want wars, let them use machines.

MORRIS

Machines break.

PUSHKY

Men die!

HELPER

Hot candle? Candle hot?

PUSHKY

(Going to HELPER)

Stop it! Stop it! You have no right!

MORRIS

The next year it was Scarlet Fever.

(The HELPER *collapses — wheezing for his life)*

PUSHKY

Seven months he lay like a corpse.

MORRIS

A corpse! A corpse! Cut up like a chicken!

PUSHKY

Moish, please. He's all I've got.

MORRIS

What about me?

PUSHKY

I need a baby.

MORRIS

Go to sleep. Take a pill.

(The HELPERS *bring down the grave-blanket and hold it in front of* PUSHKY *and* MORRIS — *making it appear as if they're in bed.* PUSHKY *looks around, bewildered. The* HELPER's *wheezing intensifies.* MONEY *and* STUD *urge* PUSHKY *to go on.)*

PUSHKY

(Helping MORRIS *to relive the past again)*

Mamele's sick. Maybe dying. Over a week, I haven't taken a pot.

MORRIS

You'll win tomorrow. He'll be all right.

PUSHKY

I feel like the time mama was dying. Stupid. Empty. A warning from God. Like something's going to happen and I can't stop it. One isn't enough, she keeps whispering from the grave. A loss like me can't be replaced so easy.

MORRIS

I'll buy you a rabbit's foot. Get some rest.

PUSHKY

What kind of man are you?

MORRIS

Very tired. I have to move the car tomorrow. Eight o'clock.

PUSHKY

What's the matter? I don't excite you? Nipples like these you don't find in dreams.

(MORRIS *looks, shrugs)*

The King of England doesn't get such a handful.

MORRIS

The King of England doesn't have to move my car.

PUSHKY

I'll blow in your ear. I'll do the other thing. Anything you want. Just don't mock the grave.

MORRIS

Pushky, please.

PUSHKY

Don't talk. Just rub.

MORRIS

What the hell am I? Some stud for the dead?

PUSHKY

Men. Men. Only when *they* want it.

HELPER

(Popping up, Mamele again)

More... More... More... More!!!

(The HELPERS *give* PUSHKY *a spoon and lead her to the* HELPER)

MORRIS

Children... Cars... Graves... Women...

(PUSHKY *starts feeding the* HELPER)

MORRIS

The more you feed them, the more they eat. . .

(Turning to PUSHKY, *finding her feeding the child)*

How much can you *schtup* him?

PUSHKY

As much as he wants!

MORRIS

How do you know how much? Can he breathe? Can he talk?

PUSHKY

He's *my* child. . .

MORRIS

What does that make *me?*

PUSHKY

Don't ask.

MORRIS

I'm warning you, Pushky. Ever since I came home, you've been hinting at something. . .

PUSHKY

He looks like you, doesn't he? What are you worried about?

MORRIS

(Out — to audience)

She was in such a hurry — to get married. . .

PUSHKY

Germany invading Russia. . . My mother-dying. . .

MORRIS

Right after the honeymoon — she sends me to the doctor...

PUSHKY

(To audience)

I had to get pregnant...

(To MORRIS)

Before they took you away.

MORRIS

Every week — I put it in a shot-glass. I got news for you. I began to look forward.

PUSHKY

I always knew there was something wrong with you.

MORRIS

It's better than I get now. Since *he* lives here. . .

PUSHKY

You don't like it. Shop elsewhere.

MORRIS

Don't think. Don't think I wouldn't.

(To audience)

Every night I come home I stop at the grocer. Buy cream... Cupcakes... a can of tuna...

(Pulling out lists)

Lists. Lists. Nothing but lists... Pick up shirts... Make a list... You think I need these things? I hate tuna. It's the brown paper-bag... I need. To make sure I go home. Where can you go with a brown paper-bag? You *have* to go home. You have no choice.

PUSHKY

Some lover.

MORRIS

Why did you marry me?

(THEY *stare at each other)*

Why *me?* If all you needed was cock?

(PUSHKY *stares at him. Then, shrugging)*

PUSHKY

You were there.

MORRIS

So was Nosebleed.

PUSHKY

(Laughing contemptuously)

Nosebleed Needleman. That's another one.

(To audience)

I'm peeing in the ocean...

MORRIS

(Suddenly ducking under PUSHKY's *legs)*

Hey, Nosebleed...

PUSHKY

(Screaming, on top of MORRIS' *shoulders)*

Put me down!

MORRIS

(To HELPER)

Look what I found!

HELPER

(Jumping off high-chair, wearing enormous codpiece)

Throw it here!

(MORRIS *throws* PUSHKY *to* HELPER (NOSEBLEED) *who catches and mounts her)*

MORRIS

That night — under the boardwalk...

HELPER (NOSEBLEED)

(Suddenly throwing his head back, holding his nose)

I'm sorry. Forgive me. I must be some kind of freak. It always happens. Just when I'm getting there...

(PUSHKY *escapes)*

MORRIS

It served you right. Falling for appearances.

PUSHKY

Madman. Torturer. Tell me where the baby is!

MORRIS

It could have been anybody. Just my luck!

PUSHKY

(To audience)

All that summer — my mother on the fire-escape... Her arms like wires... Listening to her Roosevelt... In the alley — the Super — giving it to the Knife-Man: Gonoph! Thief! Because of Jews like you, they're burning us in Poland!... Mama, please. Come in. You'll catch cold... Mamele, she called me. Her little mother... Always worrying, always looking after

PUSHKY (cont'd)

her... While my father *zitzed* himself! Steaming... stinking up the bathroom! Leaving her the droppings of his shredded corns!

MORRIS

(Into phone again)

Hello, Pushky. This is Hersch.

PUSHKY

That's when they told me. She had a year, maybe less...

MORRIS

Hersch Edelman? Remember? Rockaway?

PUSHKY

You'll live with your father. You'll get over it.

MORRIS

Nosebleed's friend. The one they call Moish.

PUSHKY

I'll kill myself first!

MORRIS

There was something about her... Some beat. Some rhythm...

PUSHKY

I was a bargain, Goddamnit!

MORRIS

The night we got married she laid it on the line:

PUSHKY

Chinese eyes. Legs that never need shaving.

MORRIS

"I give you your excitement. Then you give me mine. That way, we don't waste time and everybody gets...

PUSHKY

What are *you* complaining about? *You* got! More for your little thing than most men get in a lifetime.

MORRIS

We don't make love. We deal in trade.

PUSHKY

You don't like it... do your business elsewhere.

MORRIS

Don't think. Don't think I wouldn't...

(Again, to audience)

At school, a new teacher. Ass like melons. Brown as an almond. She calls me Herschel. In the back of the room — a young David. So cool... unafraid... No hips.

PUSHKY

Fairy. Pervert. I should have known.

MORRIS

What should I do? Sneak feels in the closet? Arrange conferences in the back of my car?

PUSHKY

The things you made me do...

MORRIS

I want what's coming...

PUSHKY

Every time I swore: Never again... Then I thought: You have to get used to it. He'll hurt the baby. Take it out on *him.*

MORRIS

Him! Him! Always *him!*

*(*HE *goes toward* HELPER *in high-chair—as if to kill him)*

PUSHKY

(Protecting child, standing in front of him)

Without *him,* you'd have gotten nothing!

MORRIS

What have I got?

PUSHKY

I gave you a Prince. A Golden God!

(HELPER *throws* MORRIS *a diary)*

MORRIS

(Looking through it, reading)

"Dear Diary. I am fat."

PUSHKY

(To HELPER)

Where did you get that?

MORRIS

(Turning pages, reading)

"Where's my penis?"

PUSHKY

(To MORRIS)

That belongs to Mamele. Give it to *me!*

MORRIS

(Reading)

MORRIS (cont'd)

"Today for my birthday mommy took me to a puppet-show. Hansel and Gretel. All about a witch. Who locks children up and stuffs them with food till they're fat enough to eat."

PUSHKY

You have no right to touch his things!

MORRIS

"Later we had sundaes, mommy and me, whipped cream and nuts and syrup all over."

PUSHKY

So what if he was plump? He had *personality!*

MORRIS

"Dear Diary... Today is my Bar-Mitzvah..."

PUSHKY

A coronation. You never saw such a table.

MORRIS

"What I don't understand is why I have hair down there when my best friend Cookie can't even get it to squirt..."

PUSHKY

You had to get him drunk... Make him dance with the band-singer...

MORRIS

"My father just told me..."

PUSHKY

We couldn't get him off her...

MORRIS

"I'm not thirteen! I'm sixteen!... My mother is a thief...

MORRIS (cont'd)

She's tried to rob me... keep me in a cage...

PUSHKY

He wouldn't listen... He wouldn't eat...

MORRIS

"I'm going away..."

PUSHKY

(To MORRIS)

Because of *you*...

MORRIS

"I'll write to my uncles... Money... Stud... I'll be a movie-star... a big tycoon..."

PUSHKY

(To audience, indicating MONEY *and* STUD*)*

They never even answered him!

MORRIS

"Nobody loves me."

PUSHKY

He wanted love he should have known where to come for it.

MORRIS

(Turning the pages ahead)

I'm going to college. . . If worse comes to worse, I can always teach — like my father."

*(*HE *stops, stares at* PUSHKY *with rage. A moment, then ripping up the diary:)*

You want him? You want to know where your precious baby is?

MORRIS (cont'd)

*(*PUSHKY *stares at him. Everyone waits, silently, tensely. Another long moment, then:)*

I put it inside... inside... inside something...

PUSHKY

Inside *what?*

STUD

Is he safe?

MONEY

Is he alive?

CROWD

Start searching... Start looking...

The CROWD *starts looking everywhere.*

MORRIS

(To STUD *and* MONEY)

Hide me, he said. Avenge my birth...

(To audience)

That night on the phone: Hello Pa. I'm pregnant. . . God fucked me. Deserted me. A child needs a father. . .

(To STUD *and* MONEY)

What did he mean? A child needs a father...

(To PUSHKY)

Tell me. The truth! Was he mine or wasn't he?

(The CROWD *stops searching, looks at* PUSHKY, *waits for the answer.)*

PUSHKY

(Quietly)
Where's the baby?

(MORRIS *stares at her. Then:)*

MORRIS

What baby? There's only a chicken.

(PUSHKY *screams, rushes for him. The* HELPER *holds her back. She weeps.*

STUD

Oh, for Christ's sake...
(To PUSHKY)
Tell him!

MONEY

Tell him!
(To MORRIS)
She'll tell you. Everything.

MONEY

Untie our hands!

(MORRIS *stares at them, then looks at the* HELPER. *The* HELPER *goes to* STUD *and* MONEY *and unties them. They all look at* PUSHKY.*)*

STUD

Tell him.

MONEY

Tell him.

STUD

Tell everybody.

MONEY

Tell the world.

(PUSHKY *looks at them, at the crowd, the audience, then at* MORRIS. *A long wait, then:)*

PUSHKY

(To MORRIS*)*

He may have been yours.

(Then shrugging, going on without apology, matter-of-factly)

Then again, maybe not... They took you overseas before I knew I was pregnant... I was desperate... frantic... nineteen... My mother had six, seven months to live, if that... I had to make sure... increase the odds... Besides, I didn't want your child. I wanted my own. With the father in doubt, he'd be all mine.

STUD

(To MORRIS, *going to huge blow-up of Mr. Everybody)*

You think this Prince could have been a son of yours?

MONEY

He was *my* son!

STUD

(To MONEY)

You!

(To MORRIS

I was his father!

MORRIS

Oh, my God! They *both* put it in the pushky!

MONEY

To STUD)

She came to *me*. . .

STUD

(To MONEY)

She came to *me!*

CROWD	**DOLL-CHILD**
Her brothers! God help her!	Enjoy your guilt!

MONEY

(To CROWD)

We're not her brothers!

STUD

(Indicating MONEY)

We're not even related. . .

(Pointing to PUSHKY)

Once her mother had *her,* she didn't want anymore. . .

MONEY

Her father wanted sons, he had to go back to the old country.

STUD

My *real* parents. . .

MONEY

My real parents. . .

STUD

. . . persecuted. . .

MONEY

. . . threatened with extermination. . .

STUD

(Pointing to PUSHKY)

. . . paid *her* father a fortune to get us out. . .

MONEY

Give us his name.

STUD

Bring us to America. . .

MONEY

As his long-lost sons!

PUSHKY

Some bargains!

MONEY

(To the CROWD)

There's no incest here. . .

STUD

Just a little adultery. . .

(Suddenly, to PUSHKY, *indicating* MONEY*)*

Tell him. . .

MONEY

(Indicating STUD)

Tell him. . . how you came to me weeping. . .

STUD

How you came to *me* — to make it all up. . .

(To CROWD)

Our father. . . the Rabbi. . . the scholar. . . the torturer. . . From the time we were little — he made her sleep between us. . .

MONEY

Willpower!

STUD

Willpower!

MONEY

Mustn't touch. If we got too close to her — he'd take off his belt and make us catch the cat.

STUD

Never... not once... did we feel the belt ourselves...

MONEY

Only through the cat...

STUD

Who suffered for *our* curiosity...

MONEY

She came to me and told *me* the same thing. . . How guilty she felt for being Mama's pet... Mama's Princess... Getting *everything* — while *we* got the left-overs.

STUD

Now...

MONEY

Now. . . that Mama was dying. . .

STUD

. . . to get even with Papa. . .

MONEY

... she'd give me what I wanted...

STUD

(Going into trance)

STUD (cont'd)

. . . what I lay there dreaming of. . .

MONEY & STUD

Every night!

STUD

(Quietly — in ecstasy)

Her hot, peppered breath. . .

MONEY

From her mother's kugel.

STUD

Her soft inside. . .

MONEY

Like her mother's bread!

MORRIS

(To PUSHKY)

You weren't ashamed?

PUSHKY

(Shrugging)

Desperate, you *do* things.

STUD

(To MORRIS)

You asked.

MONEY

We told you!

STUD & MONEY

Now give me the kid!

MORRIS

(Looking at them, then out — to audience)

I always knew. I always suspected. Her two brothers. That's all I heard. If only Mamele could have *them* for a father! A Vice-President! A King of Junk!

(To PUSHKY)

How did it feel having such big ones? How did it feel having such pricks?

(To CROWD)

Who should I give him to?

(To STUD*)*

You?

(To MONEY)

Or you?

MONEY

The *new* kid is mine. Just like the first was.

STUD

The new child is mine. He belongs to God!

MORRIS

The second Mamele — you put it in *again?*

(To PUSHKY)

Once wasn't enough? They *schtupped* you *twice?*

PUSHKY

A winning hand you don't break up.

STUD

(To PUSHKY)

Tell him.

MONEY

Tell him.

MORRIS

I don't need to hear!

(Out — to audience)

I'm fifty-three. She wants another one. Her mother — whispering again. The pot — empty. What's to lose? I thought. What could happen? She told me she was pregnant, I thought: What do you know? I'm still hot stuff!

PUSHKY

You're hot stuff!

MONEY

(Going to PUSHKY *— turning her to audience)*

If *he* won't listen, tell *them!*

STUD

(Displaying PUSHKY *to audience)*

This woman is a madonna! The new child — a miracle.

MONEY

A Victory for Science! Hope — for the Future!

STUD

(To PUSHKY)

Tell them how you came to me — just when I needed you.

MONEY

How you came to *me* — while I was still in the hospital.

STUD

(Indicating himself)

Given up for dead — cancer of the groin.

MONEY

(Indicating his body)

Every limb. Every organ. Completely transplanted!

STUD

She comes to *me* — for another baby!

MONEY

She comes to *me* — for a new Mamele.

STUD

The *first* Mamele —

MONEY

A big star now!

STUD

Mr. Everybody! Prime Time!

MONEY

Tell them...

STUD

Tell them.

MONEY

How he no longer needed you.

STUD

(Indicating WIDOW)

How — *she* — his wife — turned him against you.

(PUSHKY *looks at the* WIDOW, *then — out to audience)*

PUSHKY

I didn't recognize him. All new he looked. Up to then — a poor teacher. All of a sudden, he's on television... The father of one of his students — a big shot producer saw something in him, gave him a chance... A local show — talking to kids. Overnight — letters. From children. Old people. At long last

PUSHKY (cont'd)

— somebody we can trust. Somebody we can talk to. I wish you were my mother... my boss.. my boy friend... If only my teacher understood... listened like you do... Within six months, networks fighting... If I wanted to see him, I had to put on the television, make an appointment... His own number... His own barber...

(The HELPER *comes forward and stands before her.*

Going on, talking to HELPER *as if he were Mamele)*

Your wife likes you this way?... When do you find time?

(To HELPER/MAMELE)

All right. I'm going. Call your father sometime... Need anything?

(The HELPER *looks at her and laughs)*

What's so funny? I can still buy and sell you...

(To audience)

The last time we met, I had no pride. Right in front of me, he kept slipping away...

(Going to HELPER*)*

I don't know what's wrong. I can't take a pot. The doctor says I'm fine. I should just act normal... How can I act normal when you don't talk to me? When you don't confide in me? What's wrong? Why can't you give me a grandchild? Your grandmother's whispering... Another Mamele...

HELPER

(Turning out front, no emotion)

Tell my grandmother to go to hell. She wants a baby, let her fuck herself.

PUSHKY

How dare you insult her? Deny the grave?

HELPER

I can't deliver. Get the message?

PUSHKY

(Stunned, pointing at WIDOW)

It's all her fault.

HELPER

All mine.

PUSHKY

(Going to HELPER)

How do you know these things? Who *are* you?

(The HELPER *smiles.*

Going to WIDOW)

I must know...

Indicating the WIDOW's *belly)*

It's *his,* right? He was only punishing... trying to hurt me... Why else would he lie if he knew you were pregnant? He *did* know, didn't he? Why wouldn't you tell him? Or *did* you tell him and torment him with doubt?... I must know if my son was a man or not... Why won't she speak? ... Why doesn't she answer me? ... I'm his mother ... I've paid in blood ... Spiteful bitch! ... Why didn't you get rid of it? ... Only when *I* entered the race. . . *Then* you wanted it. . . I *still* won ... I'm *still* the winner! Do you think I wanted the belly again — at my age? It made me sick just to look at myself ... I could have been your mother ... sister ... friend ... Instead, you fought me... forced my hand...

MONEY

The timing was perfect...

STUD

A sign from God.

. MONEY

My recovery was complete, except for one last transplant...

STUD

The night before she came to me, He made his wonder known ... Thy penis is healed, He said ... Go *into* the world...

MONEY

If I could prove my dick worked, there'd be no end to me...

STUD

Make of it a conduit, connecting Man with God...

MONEY

Who walks in — but my horny sister?

STUD

As soon as she appeared, I knew God had sent her...

MONEY

The most I dreamed was to get it up...

STUD

I remember His words: *Kings* shall come of thee. . .

MONEY

A kid, Christ! That's *really* a miracle...

STUD

(To CROWD, *possessed again)*

The boy is holy! His birth is my credentials. . .

MONEY

(To STUD)

MONEY (cont'd)
Screw your credentials! He belongs to *me!*

PUSHKY
(Going to MORRIS)
Moish, please... They're both insane... Give me the baby. I'll keep him for *us.*

STUD
(Suddenly, to audience)
You be the judge.

MONEY
(To audience)
You decide!

MORRIS
Decide *what?* I'm still his father!

MONEY
(Going down to audience, standing in front of his huge blow-up)
With *me,* he'll make millions ... live forever...

STUD
(Going down to audience, standing in front of his huge blow-up)
Through *me,* he'll achieve *true* immortality.

MORRIS
(To audience)
You gonna listen to these nuts? They're crazier than I am!

MONEY
I'll give it to you straight. No crap...

(The HELPER *shushes* MORRIS *and*

takes him to the side, telling him to listen.)

MONEY

(To audience)

Two years ago, I was a smashed-up wreck. For weeks along the highway, they were picking up the pieces. A toe. A spark plug. An eyeball. A hub cap. Junk for one of my own smelters — if it wasn't for the doctor here...

(DR. DOOVER *comes up behind him, bows, gives him a shot.* MONEY *goes on, energized, matter-of-factly)*

Up until *we* got together, transplants were strictly monkey-business... See these hands? ... I used to be ashamed of them. Cracked scabby hooves from scratching at eczema... These...

(Indicates his hands)

. . . come off a corpse. . . a college basketball player. . . My guts come from Toronto — shipped frozen by jet. ... Get the picture? See what I'm driving at? ... I'm only the beginning. Another twenty years, we can *all* beat the grave. All it takes is time and a little organization... Time to build a staff, a stockpile of parts... Parts are my business. I learned their value early. Steamered up the Amazon when I was twenty-one trading flashlight batteries and tires for trinkets and pears. In fruit alone, I made a million last year... Temples in India hang my Jeep valves for decoration. Even broken glass brings in a buck. Ground it up and they line the highways with it... Name *any* part and I'll find you a customer. . . I've already signed the doctor to an exclusive long-term contract. Together we've formed a partnership, a closed-circuit network... Need a new gall bladder? Eardrum? Lung? Have your doctor call one of our dealers in every major city... You don't even have to be sick... You just need a change... Tell the truth. How many gals out there would object to a new brassiere-cup? ... How many guys would mind something "looser?" In the

MONEY (cont'd)

works right now is a deal with some movie stars. Soon as they go, we get their goods . . . There'll never be a shortage. We've got these banks. Wanna save a pancreas? Keep it stored — in a baboon. And don't forget wars — our biggest source of supply. Not H-bombs or anything — that we save for later when skin's at a premium. Till then we stick to conflicts to let the stockpile accumulate . . . to ease, to tease us — keep the peace itching . . .

(Without realizing it, HE *begins to scratch his hands.* DOOVER stands by, ready to control him)

See what I mean? . . . There's no end in sight. Just last week — I was on the phone with China — offered them cash on delivery for all their fatalities . . . I'll pay cash right now for just your signatures. . . *You* may not live to see the day when you can live forever. But your children will. You owe it to *them* — to sell me your bodies. For *their* sake, in the name of progress, I'll take skin, rib-cages, kidneys, finger-nails . . . Why feed the graveyards? I'll meet your insurance policies . . . Don't you see? The future is mine. The kid is the proof of how far I can go. . .

OLD MAN

What did he say?

MORRIS

Hubcaps? . . . Brassiere-cups? . . . Movie stars? . . . Eyeballs? . . .

STUD

(To audience)

You've heard the pitch. Now listen to me. My brother's a maniac. You know that, don't you? . . . Is this the way you see yourselves — as old cars, bathtubs, refrigerators . . . Just so much hardware for his giant machines? You really believe Einstein's brain inside you will change your thoughts? Ideas?

STUD (cont'd)

Fantasies? . . . Some movie star's crotch — your fears. Your needs. Your conscience . . . Guilt's appetite for punishment will still seek satisfaction. And what of love? Redemption? Knowledge? Pleasure? Equality? Recognition? Power? Freedom? Do *these* come with the parts? Can *they* be grafted? Man's prison is his appetite. *Not* his body. *Appetite without shame. That's* the key. In the name of my son, let me unlock you . . .

MORRIS

(Pointing to MONEY)

I thought *he* was crazy . . .

MONEY

Let him finish.

STUD

I too was a victim of my father's madness . . . When the cat got the whip, I felt guilty, cheated . . . Soon as everyone was asleep I'd sneak around the back, rip his claws along my body till I drew blood. I had to know the limits of pain . . . pleasure. My father kept telling me: "You're worth nothing." To know everything physically nourished, increased me. When I ran away from home, I walked — as far as Chicago. Drove a Judas wagon across the Plains through twenty-below. My first job in pictures was stuntman for the star. Jumping off a motorcycle at 90 miles an hour. Pleasure was harder. It came too easy. Women, alone, grew tiresome, singular. As long as there were alternatives, I could never rest. I had to know children. Animals. Objects. As soon as I knew beauty, I had to know ugliness. An old hag with sores oozing between her thighs, a corpse's asshole, his indifferent prick. You think these are limits? There *are* no depths. I came to know flowers . . . the inside of trees . . . manure . . . ice . . . the bottom of the ocean . . . One night in Pasadena at a preview of one of my pictures, a boy around twenty tried to climb the screen,

STUD (cont'd)

jumping at my close-up, sliding down my face, clutching at my lips, screaming: Let me in . . . I understood that boy. I knew his need. I wanted to tell him I was the same as he was . . . that I too needed to penetrate and *be* penetrated . . . force my way inside your skin. Only while *I* signed autographs, they carried *him* away in a straitjacket. That's when I realized why God had chosen me . . . cursed me with this appetite . . . this geek's stomach. I was your completion, the extension of your dreams. Through *me,* you could go anywhere . . . explore and screw the universe. At first, I was afraid, needed confirmation. I waited for some sign to tell me what to do. Then suddenly my career stopped. The fans were watching television. The next ten years I lived in Hell — until one night in a motel room I turned on the Late Show. There I was: Young Abraham. My first movie: *Multitude of Nations.* That night in a dream, the Lord passed through me. "Unto thy seed," He said, "have I given this land." The next morning there were calls, wires by the thousands. I knew I had been tested, forgiven, resurrected . . . My country needed me . . . my shadow still had power. It was time to give it flesh, move amongst you, make you feel it .. The rest you know as History: First Senator, then Vice-President. Then defeat and then the cancer — to test me once again.

MORRIS

(Still trying to picture it)

A corpse's asshole? Babies? Shit?

STUD

(To audience)

I am *you* . . . what you're afraid to be. All your nightmares . . . all your possibilities. . .

MORRIS

(To audience, indicating STUD)

This you'd let inside you — knowing where it's been?

MORRIS (cont'd)

(Indicating MONEY)

This — you'd sell your skin to — so he can make a bundle when the bomb falls?

STUD

(Moving out into audience with SOLDIER)

No more fear . . . No more shame . . .

MONEY

(Moving out — into audience with DR. DOOVER)

I'll take bones . . . muscles . . . glands . . . tissues . . .

STUD

Let the Kingdom of God enter *you*. . .

MONEY

Sign up.

STUD

Raise your hand.

MONEY

Get rich!

STUD

Go down!

MORRIS

(Shouting at STUD *and* MONEY *— to bring them back)*

I remember!

(STUD *and* MONEY *stop and turn)*

MORRIS (cont'd)

I remember! I left myself a note!

PUSHKY

Where is it?

MORRIS

I forgot. Wait.

(Starts searching frantically through pockets)

Call dentist . . . Mark papers . . . Pay gas . . . Open grave . . . The grave . . . The grave . . . Look inside the grave.

(The HELPER *obeys, walks to grave, bends down)*

PUSHKY

What is he doing?

CROWD

This is sacrilege. Stop him.

(HELPER *whisks away the grave blanket, and a skeleton's skull pops up — in babushka and wig with a touch of rouge)*

PUSHKY

(Screaming)

Mama! What have they done?

Slowly, the skeleton begins to rise, emerging like a car on a garage lift. First we see a coffin in the skeleton's outstretched arms, then the skeleton's belly — the hood of an old car)

MORRIS

Open the coffin.

PUSHKY

(Running to it)

No. I won't let you.

MORRIS

Open the coffin.

*(*HELPER *snaps his fingers. His* ASSISTANTS *come over and lift the lid)*

Is it there? Was I right? Did I remember where I put it?

*(*HELPER *reaches into coffin and takes out the car's generator)*

MORRIS

(In anguish)

The generator! The generator!

CROWD

Mr. Everybody's body . . . It's gone . . . It's missing . . .

MORRIS

What good is the generator without the switch?

*(*STUD *and* MONEY *run to coffin, start searching through it frantically, pulling out the car parts)*

CROWD

First the baby . . . Now *this*. . .

PUSHKY

(To MORRIS*)*

PUSHKY (cont'd)
Liar . . . Savage . . . You said you remembered. . .

MORRIS
(Searching through pockets)
Where is it? . . . Where could it be?

MONEY
(To STUD)
You sonofabitch . . . What did you do with him?

STUD
What did *I* do with him?

PUSHKY
(To STUD *and* MONEY)
You thought you could cheat me. . .

MORRIS
(Still searching)
I put it inside inside inside something. . .

STUD
Ladies and gentlemen . . . There's been a terrible crime. . .

MONEY
Go home. . .

STUD
Lock your doors. . .

WIDOW
(Speaking for the first time)
Stay where you are.

*(*THEY *all stop and turn to her. Long pause)*

WIDOW (cont'd)

My husband's body has been removed for good cause. I've seen to it myself.

PUSHKY

She's lying. It's a trick. Only *I* know where it is.

WIDOW

Last evening this letter came.

(Taking out letter, reading:)

"Your husband David is still in danger. Even now. In the grave. His Uncles plan to use his body for their own purposes . . ."

PUSHKY

(Surprised, taking out her own letter)

Last night. The same letter.

(Reading)

"Your son David is still in danger. Even now. In the grave. His Uncles plan to use his body for their own purposes. . ."

MONEY

(Going to PUSHKY)

Let me see that. . .

STUD

(Going to WIDOW)

What's going on here?

WIDOW

(Reading)

"If you wish to prevent this, I'll keep him safe for you. . ."

PUSHKY

(Reading)

"It's not too late . . . if you call this number..."

PUSHKY & WIDOW

(Reading aloud)

478-5632."

MORRIS

(A glimmer of recognition)

478-5632!

WIDOW

(Reading)

Eight p.m.

PUSHKY

(Reading)

Extension 24.

MORRIS

24! That's my number!

(Pulling out scraps)

My turn at the bakery. . . the day I was married. . . the last numbers of my zip code. . . the door of my office. . .

(HE stops)

What office? Which office?

HELPER

(Taking out key)

Your office at school.

MORRIS

(Grabbing key)

My key! My key! Where did you get this?

HELPER

I took it off your chain when you made me monitor.

MORRIS

Why? *Why?*

HELPER

(Shrugging)

I needed an office.

PUSHKY

(To HELPER)

You wrote these letters...

MONEY & STUD

Who *are* you?

MORRIS

24! Opens everything ... The door ... the closet ... the men's room ... the phone ...

(The HELPER *snaps his fingers, the* HELPERS *bring over a phone.*

Shouting at phone)

Hello ... Hello ...

HELPER

(Taking letter from PUSHKY *and handing it to* MORRIS*)*

Call this number.

PUSHKY

(To HELPER)

Where's the baby?

MORRIS

(Reading, dialing)

478-5632.

STUD

(To WIDOW)

Where's your husband?

MONEY

(To PUSHKY)

Where's the body?

(Suddenly a phone rings — somewhere in the distance. EVERYONE *stops, listens. Four or five rings, then the* HELPER *— unseen — in a corner — answers it)*

HELPER

Hello. This is a recording. I've just stepped out. If you wish to leave a message or ask a question — wait for the beep, then begin talking.

(A pause. Then a beep. THEY *all look at each other, then all at once:)*

PUSHKY

Where's the baby? Where's Mamele?

STUD & MONEY

Who are you? . . . Where's the body?

HELPER

Thank you. As soon as I get this message, I'll call you back.

(Click.

They all look at each other. MORRIS *hangs up. The phone rings immediately)*

MORRIS

(Answering it)

MORRIS (cont'd)

Hello?

*(*ALL *focus on the phone. The* HELPER *uses a megaphone to create the telephone voice)*

HELPER

What can I do for you?

MORRIS

Who *is* this?

HELPER

Who's this?

MORRIS

Herschel Edelman. Moishe Kapoyer.

HELPER

Hi, Moish. I'm the one they hired to cut up your son.

MORRIS

Who's *they?*

HELPER

Ask *them.*

MONEY

(Grabbing phone)

Give me that.

(Into phone)

Hello . . . Hello . . .

HELPER

Hi, sweetheart. How's the great new ding-dong holding up?

MONEY

Who *is* this?

HELPER

You know who.

MONEY

I don't know what you're talking about.

HELPER

Put old ocean-fucker on. Maybe *he* can explain.

(STUD *approaches phone, takes it from* MONEY)

STUD

Hello.

HELPER

Hi, old ocean-fucker. How are you?

STUD

I don't believe I've had the pleasure . . .

HELPER

Mr. Everybody's bodyguard, remember?

STUD

If you're his bodyguard, where's his body?

HELPER

Ask his old man.

MORRIS

(Grabbing phone)

Hello. Who is this?

HELPER

Don't worry, Moish. Your secret's safe.

PUSHKY

What secret?

(Grabbing phone)

You swore you'd take care of it.

WIDOW

(Grabbing phone)

You promised me they'd never get their hands on it.

STUD

(Grabbing MORRIS)

What did he mean: Ask his old man. . . ?

MORRIS

What did he mean: He's the one they hired to cut up my son?

MONEY

(Grabbing MORRIS)

Where is it?

MONEY & STUD

Where's the body?

MORRIS

Who's *they?*

(Breaking away)

Huh? Huh?

(Pointing at them, screaming)

They did it!

(PUSHKY screams, weeps)

They couldn't do it themselves. They had to hire a butcher!

MORRIS (cont'd)

(MONEY *and* STUD *look around at the* CROWD, *the audience.*

To MONEY *and* STUD)
Why? Why did he have to be murdered?

(A long wait, then:)

STUD
The boy was dangerous.

MONEY
Out of his mind.

(THEY *start to walk toward* MORRIS *—forcing him backward)*

STUD
A threat to the *new* child.

MONEY
A threat to the future!

STUD
When his mother became pregnant, I went to him and told him — how the *new* child was conceived . . . his own beginning. Together, we could be a team. . . a Holy Trinity. . . Mr. Everybody. The *new* child. Stud Moses — their father.

MONEY
I went to him, too. Laid it on the line. Offered him a partnership in the name of Unity. Mr. Everybody. The *new* kid. Uncle Money — their daddy. A winning combination. We couldn't be beat.

PUSHKY

(To STUD *and* MONEY)

You just wanted to get even ... take them *both* away from me...

STUD

He told me I was crazy...

MONEY

Called me a ghoul...

STUD

Threatened to have his *own* kid...

MONEY

Go in business for *himself*...

WIDOW

(Contemptuously)

Another son of God. To compete with *theirs.*

PUSHKY

It *is* his! I *knew* it!

WIDOW

It *may* be his!

(Looking at PUSHKY, *smiling, then shrugging and imitating her)*

Then again — maybe not.

PUSHKY

(Screaming)

Mama! Mama! What does she want from me?

*(*SHE *rushes to the* WIDOW *and starts to shake her. The* CROWD *separates them, the* WIDOW *stands there defiantly)*

WIDOW

(To PUSHKY)

No child of mine will be a God! Some tribal sacrifice to fatten your dead.

(To MORRIS, *indicating* PUSHKY*)*

Her belly drove him crazy. He saw it as punishment. As soon as he didn't need her, she replaced him with a new child.

(Pointing to MORRIS)

In place of his father...

(Pointing to STUD *and* MONEY)

... she gave him *them.*

(Pointing to her belly)

I gave him this. . . but he wouldn't believe it was his. . . How could he?

(Pointing to PUSHKY)

With *her* for a mother — all women were liars. Instead of me, he turned to his fans ... Filled with disgust, he started to gorge himself. Within a month, he was fat, bloated. The network had to cancel him, schedule re-runs. One night, hysterical, he ran naked through the house, screaming: I have no father ... I have no son ... My wife. My mother. *Both* with bellies ... Empty of *me* ... Empty of *me*...

MONEY

The boy was in agony. He needed help.

STUD

I spoke to God. He told me what to do.

MONEY

Alive, he was finished. Dead, just beginning.

STUD

"In return for thy new child, thou must sacrifice the other!"

MONEY

Mr. Everybody's eyes ... Lips ... Crotch ...

STUD

"Deliver him divided so I may pass through him. . . !"

MONEY

His heart alone would be worth a million!

STUD

"Erect a shrine of his parts for touching and healing. . . "

MONEY

He had to go!

STUD

In the name of God!

MONEY

In the name of Science!

STUD

Humanity!

MONEY & STUD

Civilization!

PUSHKY

Murderers!

WIDOW

Vultures!

MORRIS

Who'd cut him up like that?

(THEY ALL *look at the phone.* MORRIS *rushes to it.*

Shouting)

MORRIS (cont'd)

Hello... Hello... !

HELPER

(Behind them now, quietly — in his own voice)

I never laid a hand on him.

*(*THEY ALL *turn — confused)*

PUSHKY

Who said that?

WIDOW

He's here...

(The HELPER *smiles at them)*

HELPER

I didn't have to.

PUSHKY

Who are you?

STUD

What do you want?

MONEY

What's your game?

HELPER

I'm here to be of help. And to collect for my services.

WIDOW

Where's my husband?

PUSHKY

Where are my children?

MONEY

The punk *I* hired had brown hair. . .

(HELPER *removes his wig, revealing his own hair)*

STUD

Mine had no mustache. . .

(HELPER *removes his mustache.* MORRIS *cries out)*

MORRIS

(Recognizing him)

He is one of my students!

(To audience)

Last winter, out of nowhere, he takes a seat in the back. . . Says he just wants to visit. . . get an education. . . What should I do? Throw him out? . . . The other students sit there. Morons. Zombies. This one's different. He wants to learn.

(The HELPER *smiles)*

PUSHKY

(Going to him)

Please! What have you done with the baby?

MONEY

Grabbing MORRIS)

Is he alive?

STUD

(Grabbing MORRIS)

Or isn't he?

HELPER

Leave him alone.

HELPER (cont'd)

(Silence, then:)

You'll find out everything. First the cash. Drop it in the coffin. What we each agreed to.

STUD

Why should I pay if you didn't kill him?

HELPER

I said: You'd get what's coming. You'll get what I promised.

MONEY

How can *I* get it — if you promised it to them?

HELPER

Only the Shadow knows . . . Put up or shut up.

PUSHKY

(Running over with mah jong case, emptying it into coffin)

All my winnings!

(Taking off mink and throwing it in)

This, too!

MONEY

Half now. The rest later.

(HELPER *signals to the* OTHER HELPERS — *who take off their disguises and pull out their knives)*

MORRIS

(Recognizing them)

My Higher Horizons class!

MONEY

You got some school there.

MONEY (cont'd)

(HE *throws his money into the coffin, too.* HELPER *looks at* STUD. STUD *does the same.* HELPER *looks at* WIDOW. SHE *follows suit. Long pause. Then the* HELPER *rises)*

HELPER

Dearly beloved. . . Let us pray. . .

(STUDENTS *come over and stand at each end of coffin)*

Mr. Everybody did not die in vain. He paid off double and split again.

STUDENTS

(Full soprano)

Hallelujah!

(Then bass)

Amen.

MORRIS

(To HELPER, *confused, indicating* STUD *and* MONEY)

You were working for *them* — all the time. . .

HELPER

(To MORRIS)

One morning at school your son came to see you . . . You weren't there . . . You were stuck on the highway . . . We had a talk. He was crazy, incoherent . . . all about his uncles trying to kill him — out of fear, jealousy — now that he was pregnant . . . I tried to calm him down, offered to help him . . . He hired me as his bodyguard — to protect him and his baby . . .

(Pointing to STUD *and* MONEY*)*

That's how *they* found me . . . following *him* . . . Without the

HELPER (cont'd)

other knowing it, they each hired me to kill him, cut him up, deliver his body.

WIDOW

(Ironically)

Mr. Everybody's bodyguard . . . Mr. Everybody's killer . . .

(HELPER *smiles at her, tips an imaginary hat)*

HELPER

(Going on)

The night he died, I followed him *here*. . .

(HE *indicates grave)*

. . . stood over *there* . . .

(HE *indicates trees)*

. . . watching over him . . . waiting to kill him . . .

MORRIS

But you said you *didn't* kill him . . . Who *did?*

HELPER

(Smiling)

I'll let *him* tell you that. . .

(Putting his finger to his lips)

Shhh. . . Listen. . .

(Suddenly, a voice from inside the skeleton's mouth, whispered, hushed, amplified — filling up the theatre)

MR. EVERYBODY'S VOICE

Grandma . . . Grandma . . . Is that you?

CROWD

What's that?

PUSHKY

Mamele's voice.

CROWD

Mr. Everybody!

MORRIS

(Pointing to skeleton)

Inside! The mouth!

HELPER

He's trying to tell you something.

MR. EVERYBODY'S VOICE

It's *me,* David . . . Your grandson Mamele . . . I've come back to the source . . . the scene of the crime . . . What's that? . . . Who's there? . . . Somebody's following me . . . Grandma, quickly, let me in . . . It's *me,* David . . .

(The HELPER *comes forward and speaks along with the voice simultaneously — until gradually we are listening to the* HELPER — MR. EVERYBODY's *voice — an echo — underneath)*

HELPER & VOICE

Don't you recognize me? . . . I'm a woman now . . . It's all been arranged — from the very beginning . . . David for Deborah . . . created in your image . . . Mamele . . . little Mother . . . to fill a space . . . Hurry! I feel it coming! The baby! Arms. Legs. Kicking. Spreading. . . Who's that? . . . I know you're there . . . Don't come any closer. I have a knife. I even have a tape-recorder — to record *everything.* My diary, too! To get it all down . . . Speak up if you're there . . . Tell me who you are . . . Stud? Money? My wife? My mommy? My fat mommy — who I can't make skinny . . . my skinny

HELPER & VOICE (cont'd)

wife who I didn't make fat . . . Only *mine's* a God! . . . Do you hear me, Grandma? It happened in the bathtub. . . lying in the water . . . My face in front of me pre-recorded on tape sitting on the toilet talking from a box . . . Eighty million people in the bathtub with me. They want my forgiveness . . . my love . . . my strength . . . I rise like a tree . . It isn't enough . . . I *pull* . . . I *stretch* . . . Stupid bastards! How much do you want? . . . Forgive *yourselves* . . . Forgive each other! . . . Over my feet . . . the running faucet . . . I hear its outpour under the water . . . "It's not all your fault . . . It's not all my fault . . . " God's voice in the box — out of *me,* the toilet . . . I feel His power gushing toward me . . . Oh God . . . Oh God . . . I feel His power . . .

(A moment, then quietly:)

Unborn children float over my belly. I watch them drown . . . dissolve. . . disappear. . . Oh, God. Oh, God. It wants to come out. Where? How? I can't find the opening . . . Daddy. Help me. Why aren't you here? Mommy, please. I don't want to die. If I die, you die. If you die, I die. Eat, Mamele, eat. Grow strong. Live forever!

PUSHKY

Turn it off! Turn it off!

(Pause. Then:)

HELPER & VOICE

I feel a hand. Inside my chest . . . Oh God . . . oh God . . . Where's the knife? Where's the opening? I feel his fingers . . . toes . . . cock . . . It wants to kill me . . . GET IT OUT!

(MORRIS *completes his son's scream and lunges for the skeleton, pulling out its tongue — a handful of tape which* HE *rips apart)*

MORRIS

(Screaming, weeping)

He killed himself! He killed himself! . . . I could have saved him — but it wouldn't start . . . In the morning — ten minutes . . . In the cold a half-hour. . .

(HELPER *goes to him, holds him in his arms.* MORRIS *weeps, sobs like a baby)*

HELPER

(To EVERYBODY, *indicating* MORRIS)

I was still there in the shadows when he finally arrived. Five minutes earlier and it wouldn't have happened. Soon as he left, I robbed the grave of the knife, the diary, the tape-recorder. The body I stole — after the burial — after *she* —

(Indicating PUSHKY)

— jumped in and gave birth to the *new* one.

MORRIS

That night on the phone he tried to tell me: They want my body. They want to kill me.

PUSHKY

(To MORRIS, *quietly)*

He hated us both. He did it to punish us.

MORRIS

(To PUSHKY)

I wanted to love him. You wouldn't let me.

(PUSHKY *starts to weep)*

HELPER

(To STUD *and* MONEY, *indicating* MORRIS)

HELPER (cont'd)

I brought him the body and told him what you wanted it for. He came up with the plan to help me deliver it.

MORRIS

I had this dream. This clear vision. No more children to feed the grave.

STUD

Where is the body?

MONEY

What did you do with it?

MORRIS

(Simply)

I threw it in the garbage and burned it to ashes.

PUSHKY

Oh God! Oh God!

WIDOW

David! David!

MONEY

Then *what?*

STUD

(Eagerly)

Where are his ashes?

MORRIS

I put them inside inside inside something. . .

MONEY

Inside *what?*

STUD

Inside *what?*

(MORRIS *looks at them, trying to remember. The* HELPER *snaps his fingers and the car-hood-pregnant belly of the skeleton pops open.* MONEY *and* STUD *run to the hood. One of the* HELPERS *stops them with a switchblade.* ANOTHER HELPER — dressed as a nurse — reaches into the hood and takes out the baby)

PUSHKY

(Screaming)

Mamele . . . Mamele. . .

CROWD

The baby . . . The baby. . .

(PUSHKY *runs over and takes the baby from the* NURSE)

PUSHKY

His eyes are open. He's gagged. He's breathing . . .

(Unwrapping him)

Mama's here now. They can't hurt you.

(Removing the gag, SHE *lets out a scream)*

STUD

(Running over)

His mouth!

MONEY

Stuffed with ashes!

MORRIS

I remember! I remember!

(The HELPER *takes baby from* PUSHKY *and gives him to* MORRIS *who removes the blanket)*

Holding up the baby — revealing a gaping hole in place of the child's penis — still bleeding, tied at the source)

I chopped it up and put it inside . . .

(Turning to PUSHKY, MONEY *and* STUD*)*

You! and *You!* and *You!* . . . Inside your food! Inside your bellies! To *stop* the schtupping. . . *stop* the Mameles. . . *stop* the children born in the grave. . .

(PUSHKY *screams.* STUD *and* MONEY *back away in horror. The* HELPER *gives the band the signal to start playing — then forms the* CROWD *into a circle, making them dance around* PUSHKY, MONEY *and* STUD.

Shouting over music, to audience)

Play . . . Dance . . . Weep . . . Eat . . . The power is in *you* . . . not your children . . . The power is in *you* — not your machines. . . The power is in *you* — not your money. . . The power is in *you* — not your Gods!

WIDOW

(Clutching her stomach, feeling the beginnings of birth)

Now! Now! Now it can be his!

MORRIS

(Clutching his baby, weeping, rocking)

The cycle is ended! Free! Free!

The music quickens and the dance accelerates. The CROWD *continues to dance around* PUSHKY, MONEY *and* STUD *— as the* HELPER *jumps on the gravestone above them and snaps his fingers. The skeleton flies out of the grave, flowers pop up everywhere, and the huge blow-up of Mr. Everybody smiles. Jumping down, the* HELPER *goes to get the Caterer's Wagon and brings it back on. The* OTHER HELPERS *reach into the coffin and wave the money. Throwing it in again, they close the lid and load the coffin on the wagon. The* HELPER *jumps on the wagon and waves to the audience. A last look — at* MORRIS *— who stands there clutching the baby — weeping and rocking — then the* HELPER *snaps his fingers and the wagon goes off. The play ends. The music and dancing go on...)*

The House of Edelman

Aaron Edelman,
Watchmaker

Rose Edelman,
Saint

Herschel Edelman,
English & Dramatics Teacher,
called Morris Upside-Down
(Moishe Kapoyer)

having met in the Atlantic Ocean,
Rockaway, Long Island
and
married in the Bronx, New York

Ann Edelman,
Widow
of
Mr.
Everybody

David Edelman,
(deceased)
called Mr. Everybody
(famed T.V. Star),
also called Mamele
(Little Mother)—
for his dead grandmother—
in whose grave
he was born

The House of Mazeldich

Myron Mazeldich,
Rabbi

Deborah Mazeldich,
Saint

Netta Mazeldich,
called Pushky,
the Mah Jong Queen

Manny Mazeldich,
called Uncle Money,
the King of Junk

Moses Mazeldich,
called Stud Moses,
former Film-Star
and
United States
Vice-President

the *new* David Edelman,
also called Mamele
(Little Mother)—
born eight days ago in
his brother David's grave.